How to Profit from Flower and Herb Crafts

Ellen Spector Platt

STACKPOLE BOOKS

For Margaret J. Lydic,
My Fairy Godmother

Published by
STACKPOLE BOOKS
5067 Ritter Road
Mechanicsburg, PA 17055

Printed in the United States of America

10 9 8 7 6 5 4 3 2 1

First Edition

Cover design by Kathleen D. Peters
Cover photograph by Doug Nicotera

Library of Congress Cataloging-in-Publication Data

Platt, Ellen Spector.
    How to profit from flower and herb crafts / Ellen Spector Platt. — 1st ed.
      p.   cm.
    Includes bibliographical references and index.
    ISBN 0-8117-2448-4
    1. Handicraft industries—Management.   I. Title.
HD2341.P536   1996
745.92'068—dc20
                               96-12968
                               CIP

❧ CONTENTS ❧

❧ INTRODUCTION ❧

During a recent interview on the origins of my flower and herb business, I flashed back to myself at age eight selling flowers at a little street-corner stand—jelly jars filled with water, bunches of flowers snipped from our small garden mixed with wildflowers plucked from adjacent lots. My customers consisted of kindly neighbors and passersby with a nickel to spare for a bunch of buttercups, violets, or marigolds. The adults in my large family were my most loyal customers. Surely my father was the only truck mechanic in Philadelphia who left for work with a zinnia boutonniere pinned to his coveralls.

My career path led not to horticulture, however, but to a degree in psychology and much fulfilling work teaching, researching, and counseling; my personal path led toward marriage, three children, and a hobby in pottery, with only a smattering of gardening.

In Pottsville, Pennsylvania, where I lived, if you were interested in taking part in an activity, you likely would have to help make it happen. When a few people got together to start an arts center, I got involved more out of self-interest than philanthropy. I desperately wanted the use of a high-fire gas kiln for my pottery and instruction beyond what I could get in books. Before long, the Schuylkill County Council of the Arts opened an Arts and Ethnic Center in a donated building and was able to provide studio space to several artisans at the beginning stages of their careers. As often happens, the people who work and speak up are pressed into office, and I wound up president of the council.

Several years later, our children off at college, my husband and I moved to an old stone farmhouse on the outskirts of the tiny town of Orwigsburg. It was an impulsive decision, impelled by the romantic notion of restoring a property being threatened by a developer. With the house came a huge, five-bay horse barn.

In my new surroundings, I fell into the habit of working in the garden after office hours until dark. Pulling weeds after being immersed in other people's woes allowed the daily stress to drain away. Soon I found myself racing home to the garden not wanting to leave it. My husband, a nongardener, planted my first cutting garden as a gift. I experienced the delight of having armloads of flowers to cut and play with. Soon I had more than I could possibly scatter throughout my home. After giving some away, I took my first tentative steps toward a business. I had no business plan, no goals beyond what I wanted to do in my garden that day, and no training in horticulture or business.

Selling dried flowers allowed me to maintain an office schedule and merchandise flowers on my own terms, when I had time. My fantasy was to throw the stoneware pottery that would serve as custom-made containers for my dried flower arrangements. In my naivete, I thought I could make the pots, grow the flowers, design the arrangements, market them, and still make a profit. It took me about two weeks to realize the impossible amount of time it would take to perform each segment of the operation myself. My pottery wheel has since gathered dust in my barn, spiders spinning webs from pedal to mud tray.

I cut down the hours in my office. My grand experiment began. I contacted three other craftswomen I knew from the arts center and we planned a one-day open house in the barn for selling our work. We papered the community with fliers and distributed them to our friends, neighbors, and local businesses.

Our venture was a success. People came and bought from all of us. At one point we had a traffic jam in the meadow and one of us had to go out and direct traffic. With a tidy profit for the day, my growing addiction was fed. By the time I quit my day job and went full-time into the flower and herb business, I had already learned by sweet-and-sour trial and error many of the lessons in this book. Perhaps I can save you some of the headaches and direct you to some of the excitement of being in business for yourself.

CHAPTER ONE

From Hobby to Business: Finding Your Niche

Was your first sale to a friend or coworker? Was it someone who saw a garland you made for your fireplace at Christmas and asked for one just like it? But she wanted it in her colors and with the ribbon a little longer and no cockscomb because it reminded her of brains. She was happy to pay for it, but she didn't want to pay too much. Your first retail custom order! She loved it; you probably were content just to cover the cost of materials with a little bit on the side. That first sale launched you into business.

Now you want to sell more, leave your full-time job, and make enough money from flowers and herbs to support yourself. Within the flower and herb field there are many different businesses:

• Growing and selling potted herb plants and flats of flowers for drying—a nursery business
• Growing and selling fresh cut flowers and herbs at roadside stands or farmers' markets
• Buying a retail florist business or starting one from scratch and incorporating many of your homegrown materials into your designs to make them look more natural and less commercial

- Selling flowers and edibles to restaurants and providing their fresh flowers weekly

In this book I concentrate on those who primarily want to grow or buy herbs and flowers and fashion them into glorious arrangements. You are adding value and price to the materials by the ways you form them into individual pieces. Many of the same ideas apply to those designing with silk flowers, herbs, and fruits.

It is wise to seek a specialty or niche that will set you apart from other craftspeople. Even if you have a general flower and herb business, you'll reap extra benefits by concentrating your efforts in one of these market niches. For each niche, it means reading the professional literature in that field, attending specialized conferences, and pitching marketing and promotional efforts to a specific target audience.

THE BRIDAL NICHE

After the slew of nontraditional weddings (and nonweddings) in the sixties and seventies, brides have returned to a more traditional approach with some new twists. According to the Association of Bridal Consultants, the bridal business is a $33-billion-a-year industry in the United States, with floral sales representing 4.6 percent of that amount. Flowers star at every phase of the nuptials. From shower decorations and favors to centerpieces for the rehearsal dinner, corsages, boutonnieres, and bouquets for the bridal party, massive arrangements for the house of worship, and adornments for the reception, flowers are considered a necessary part of the tradition.

Although fresh flowers are selected most frequently, dried flowers, herbs, and silk flowers are gaining in popularity because of their longevity. Brides select them because they serve the dual function of decoration and gifts to the wedding party or guests. If arranged by a professional, they are probably not going to be cheaper than fresh materials. But many brides and their families yearn for the pleasure and financial savings of arranging their own flowers on their own schedule. Design decisions can be made months in advance, materials purchased, and a group gathered to help with constructing the arrangements.

You can help brides by showing them photos of wedding work you have fashioned, by helping them with design and construction necessities, even if they will do most of the work themselves. Offer headpieces for the bride and bridal party from fresh, dried, or silk flowers, or combinations of the three. Trim lovely straw hats with flowers in the wedding colors. If you sell not only flowers but also foam, containers, tape, and bouquet holders, you can assist a bride with all her needs. If you are designing but not constructing, you must add a design fee for your time.

I offer the service of drying bridal bouquets; there is no one else in my locale providing this service. Many of the referrals come from florists, since I haven't met one yet who wants to do this and all are delighted that their work will be preserved.

Preservation requires taking the bouquets apart, drying most flowers in silica gel, knowing which will air dry effectively and which, like Baker fern, must be pressed, spraying with a sealant after the drying process is complete, and then reconstructing an arrangement.

I work only by prior appointment; brides must reserve time in advance so that I am not inundated beyond my capacity on popular weekends or on my vacation weekends. I can also find out what types of flowers brides will be using and what colors. I educate them on what to expect when these flowers are dried, such as changes in color and the inevitable shrinkage as the flowers undergo dehydration, and on the future care of the piece. I explain how to care for the flowers until the bouquet is delivered to me and set up an appointment for the delivery, which is usually done by Mom the next day. If the bouquet is small, I often request some additional flowers, like a table centerpiece or bridesmaid's bouquet.

Brides can choose several design styles: reconstruction into a wedding-style bouquet to be placed under a bell jar; a bouquet in a glass-enclosed shadowbox frame; a floral wreath, sometimes augmented by additional flowers; or even a heart-shaped wreath for over the bed.

The price of the finished arrangement is always established in advance, based on the size of the original bouquet and the style of dried design chosen. I obtain a deposit for the work, the rest to be paid upon completion. I write a pickup date on the receipt since, like the dry cleaners, I can't be responsible for items held longer than thirty days. Believe it or not, one bride who paid a deposit two years ago still hasn't picked up her bouquet. Did her marriage go sour right after the honeymoon?

The bridal niche can include pressing flowers to decorate wedding invitations and mats for wedding pictures. Such mats make a popular gift for the couple, particularly those who have everything. Since I'm not a framer, I prefer to sell the mats protected by shrink wrap and allow the giver to select her own frame. When requested, I go to a local framer from whom I get a slight discount and choose the frame. I must then charge a fee for my time in providing this service. The mats I use are all standard frame sizes (8 by 10, 11 by 14, etc.) so the giver can choose a ready-made frame and complete it herself. If you care to invest in the merchandise, carry your own line of simple frames for selection.

When people found out I was preserving bridal flowers, they started to make other requests. I've had requests to dry Valentine and birthday flowers, prom corsages, and other special occasion arrangements. I won't work with flowers that are old and brown around the edges, because the customer will be wasting her money, and we will both be dissatisfied with the results. I will, however, make a special custom potpourri of the passé flowers. When the first person asked me to dry funeral flowers sent at her father's death, I was somewhat taken aback. But the process is no different than for wedding flowers. Betty brought me five funeral baskets and I picked the best flowers from each to dry. She decided on a heart-shaped wreath, and we were both pleased with the results.

My latest request to preserve remembrance flowers was from a mother and daughter whose husband and father had just died. He was an avid gardener, had planted a patch of sunflowers, and hadn't lived to see them bloom. The mother selected a sunflower wreath and a small arrangement on a dried sunflower seed head; the daughter selected a sunflower picture in a shadowbox frame. I added some of my own dried flowers with the permission of the customers to augment the design, but the sunflowers predominated.

My special promotional piece to advertise my service is shown here. I included it in several issues of the biannual newsletter and circulated it to florists and bridal shops. I hand painted the roses with a watercolor wash to add to the appeal.

If you grow your own flowers without pesticides, consider cake decorating with fresh or dried flowers as part of the services you offer. Most florist flowers are heavily sprayed with pesticides before they ever reach the florist and using them with food is risky. Yours would be a novel service.

Host your own open house, a tea, or other event

for brides at which you can demonstrate your wares. If your house lends itself to the occasion, take over several rooms and completely decorate for weddings, using several different themes and color schemes in different areas. Invite other businesses to exhibit with you, sharing the cost of advertising and the work of promotion.

If you want to find a niche in the bridal market, consider joining the Association of Bridal Consultants (see references at the back of the book for the address), which includes specialists in all aspects of wedding sales. Their literature, educational materials, and regional and national conferences will help you to further your goals in the wedding business.

Most large and many small cities offer opportunities to participate in retail bridal shows. The shows themselves may be produced by promoters, newspapers, magazines like *Modern Bride*, hotels, or a group of retail businesses themselves. You may want to join a bridal show in your area and have a booth to publicize your services. To find out where and when these shows are, call the advertising department of your newspaper and ⟜ **ask the ad reps who will know when and where the shows are.*** They will try to sell you advertising space in their next bridal issue. Gather whatever information they have and consider it well. Check out the show in the same ways that you research flower and crafts shows.

Since the attendees will be brides, their mothers, and friends (future brides?), you're marketing to a highly selective audience. It makes no sense to display at a show fifty miles away where customers will not drive to your shop for services. Since you are selling future services, rather than products on the spot, your display and literature must be of the quality to represent you well.

For direct mail marketing, look for listings of engagements in the local newspapers and send your literature to the bride-to-be.

---

* You must be assertive if you are to get the help and information you need to develop your business. Throughout this book, I emphasize—in the above manner—those moments when it is crucial to be bold and confident when asking for something.

She will be inundated with advertisements from other establishments, photographers, caterers, and bridal shops. Make your brochure stand out by its design and the quality of the paper.

Peruse the bridal magazines like *Brides & Your New Home* and *Modern Bride* regularly to see what the trends are in colors, flowers, wedding themes, and bridal gowns. Talk to local bridal shop owners and see how their experiences compare with the national trends. Arrange to place an example of your work in the shop in a way that will also enhance the shop display.

CORPORATE AND COMMERCIAL ACCOUNTS

Have you ever walked into a bank before Easter and seen cardboard cutouts of chicks and eggs taped to the office walls? The office staff is making an attempt to decorate with a holiday theme. You loved it in second grade, but not in a place of business; likely as not, the bank doesn't love it either and would appreciate your help decorating with more sophisticated and businesslike designs. Businesses buy floral arrangements with which to decorate their lobbies and offices. Offer seasonal arrangements and an installation service whereby you bring and place everything and remove the old materials. That way the office staff needn't be bothered, and management has more control over the aesthetics of the project.

Some companies buy floral gifts for their clients to celebrate a success or the opening of a new venture. Offer to scout the decor and to design something in the appropriate shape, size, color, and budget.

Businesses buy more and more items for Secretaries Week. Remind your clients of the date well in advance and help them choose items within their budget. They will thank you for the reminder and for the fact that your dried or silk arrangements have some permanence and won't be tossed by the end of the week.

Special dinners, Christmas parties, and new-product launches are all occasions for floral designs. Sometimes a small favor for each person, clustered together as a decoration and later retrieved to take home, is most appreciated.

Check with hotels and restaurants about their regular floral needs or their special needs at holiday times. Working with dried and silk materials means that decorations can be partially or completely made before the holiday, helping you to cope with the onslaught of orders.

Approach professional organizations and businesses that organize and produce conferences and meetings. They can be excellent sources of orders for special occasion designs. The organizer may be looking for an original "spouse program," a euphemism for women's program, while the members of the organization are attending professional meetings.

Recently, my dentist was organizing a five-county, day-long meeting for the state dental society. He asked me for workshop suggestions and I typed up a proposal with three ideas, at three cost levels. He selected one and it was included in the written program sent in advance to all the dentists. A wonderful group of women came to my barn for a hands-on workshop on how to make potpourri. They took home bags of what they had made, along with instructions, and spent some time shopping in the barn before they joined their husbands for lunch. Now I offer lunch and teas, cooking and baking with herbs and my own or local fresh produce in season, as part of a workshop to extend the floral experience.

To succeed in this niche, establish your credentials by joining the local chamber of commerce and the local business association. Attend their meetings and functions where people are expected to tell each other about their businesses to make contacts for future business. Offer to work on a committee that is relevant to you. Use their membership lists for targeted marketing.

DECORATING HOMES FOR CHRISTMAS AND OTHER SPECIAL EVENTS

Christmas is big business and as more and more women enter the work force, they often don't have the time to decorate as they used to or as they wish to. Your special niche can be aimed toward holiday parties. Like the bridal niche, it involves meetings with the clients, exploring themes and designs, making choices, and, finally, installations. For Christmas it may involve decorating outside and in, even trimming the tree. Ask about special events to be held at the home, like a holiday open house or Christmas Eve party, and design appropriate decorations, centerpieces, and favors for the occasion and for various spots in the house. Offer additional suggestions, from a refreshing holiday potpourri in the powder room to large topiaries in floor pots offering a special greeting in the foyer or outside entryway.

Remind clients that Christmas isn't the only season of the year to decorate. From the important anniversary party to the fundraiser for the hospital, people want to put special effort into a major floral decorating scheme. Suggest that you are available.

When your local library is having its spring house-and-garden tour or its fall decorators' showcase, offer to do the flowers for one house or one room. This involves working with the committee to produce something within its guidelines and having quantities of literature available for visitors to pick up. How do you know that this expensive and time-consuming venture will generate more business for you? Make it a practice to ask new clients how or where they heard about you. You'll soon find out whether your participation was worthwhile. Often you will hear that someone's friend saw your work in a particular home. That counts!

TOTALLY HERBAL

Herbs continue to grow in popularity, for culinary uses like teas, flavorings in jams and vinegars, and cooking; for medicinal purposes, both taken internally and used as skin balms and soothing bath products; for aromatic purposes, including aroma therapy and potpourris; and in dried decorations. There is an increased interest in herbal weddings and in combining herbs in fresh and dried flower bouquets. A shop devoted exclusively to interest in herbs fills a very popular niche. In her charming book *Growing an Herb Business*, Bertha Reppert provides an informative discussion of the ways her business, Rosemary House in Mechanicsburg, Pennsylvania, grew from a small one-person, home-based business to a large family enterprise.

CULINARY CONCERNS

Try an herb shop tipped in the culinary direction. An interest in culinary herbs and flowers leads to developing and publishing recipes, teaching cooking classes, writing cookbooks, planting a demonstration garden, offering tastings, and leading tours to fine restaurants where chefs specialize in growing and cooking their own herbs and edible flowers. The Marx Bros. restaurant in Anchorage, Alaska, is one such place, a treat for any herb aficionado.

A culinary emphasis leads to designing table centerpieces, kitchen wall hangings of all kinds, napkin rings, and chair back designs for special parties; cooking and baking your own herbal products; making your own spice mixes; and packing culinary gift baskets.

When dealing with edibles, be sure to check on state and local food regulations. Call the Department of Agriculture and your state extension agent before you get started. You will probably need to have your kitchen inspected regularly and follow a host of other regulations, certainly doable, but you want no surprises. Check also on necessary liability insurance.

In seeking shows to display and sell your wares, look for "Book and Cook" type shows, which attract gourmands. A famous one in Philadelphia, a charity event produced by the local PBS station, features famous chefs and cookbook authors with vendors of all types of food-related products.

Your display theme at any show will include cooking and table-top items, indicating your special interest in culinary products.

TOURING

Some artisans in the flower and herb field have added a touring component to their businesses. Betsy Williams of The Proper Season in Andover, Massachusetts, has a yearly roster of foreign and domestic tours as well as learning vacations featuring herbs and flowers. For each tour she plans a complete itinerary and visits in advance when possible. Her customers eagerly await her annual list of destinations, often combining the famous with lesser-known gems. The tours are both an adjunct to her shop business, drawing in new customers interested in her dried flower products, and a profit center in themselves.

FRESH FLOWERS AND HERBS FOR DECORATING
Dried flowers and herbs sit neatly on the shelf until you are ready to arrange and sell them; many floral artists, however, carve a niche for themselves using fresh materials exclusively. Whether in Manhattan working from a cramped apartment or in Boise working from a skylit studio, designers usually start with parties and special events. Perhaps it all begins when a friend admires the unusual arrangements at your parents' anniversary party and asks you to create something spectacular for a second marriage.

This niche differs from that of the traditional full-service florist, who sells a full line of cash-and-carry arrangements or flowers by the stem, and whose truck delivers to the local hospitals at least once a day. It's also different from a wire service that sends and receives orders from around the world. A custom flower arranger works by appointment only.

Donna Lee Holmes of Hollis, New Hampshire, supplements income from a part-time job with a fresh flower design business called Hollis-Holmes. Word-of-mouth advertising generates as many clients as she can handle. She uses her distinctive busi-

HOLLIS-
HOLMES
FLORAL
DESIGN

DONNA LEE
HOLMES
FIFTY-TWO
TWISS LANE
HOLLIS
NH 03049
603 465 3775

ness cards at each job as her sole form of advertising. Donna buys most of her flowers from the Flower Exchange in Boston, a major wholesale market, and supplements her purchases with flowers from her garden and from nearby woods and roadsides.

In a fresh flower design business, appointments are made to discuss the project, to see the space where the flowers will be placed, and to deliver and install the flowers. Sometimes the creation is done totally on site; sometimes the materials are prearranged and delivered ready to use. Because this type of custom business is by appointment, you have some control over your schedule and can refuse work at certain busy times if the orders threaten to become overwhelming. Since this is a custom business, your prices must reflect the time it takes to meet with the customer and to design the flowers in a unique way. For example, florists may take a 20 percent markup for labor on everyday work and at least a 35 percent markup for labor on wedding work. For a wedding you may meet with the bride and her mother once to present your ideas; they may think it over and come back to make a selection. Then the bride calls to change the number in the wedding party; in yet another call her mother-in-law-to-be has a special request for a wrist corsage, and then numbers must change one more time. Custom work can actually lose you money if you don't take into account the extra time involved and perhaps the time researching special containers and effects (see chapter 10 on pricing). Custom work can often start and be done out of the home, so there is a savings on overhead to balance out the extra costs. There can be less waste if you plan and order carefully, because you know in advance how much you need.

Using flowers solely from local wholesale distributors means selecting creative combinations and colors. It means establishing a relationship with your wholesaler so that he will order anything you request, with sufficient notice. It means checking out your local farmers' market for sparkling fruits, fresh herbs, and vegetables to combine with the flowers to supplement overused species like mums and carnations.

If you live outside of the reach of a wholesaler with a superb selection, you may need to look elsewhere for interesting material. A few wildflowers or branches from woody ornamentals, even trees, change the entire look of an arrangement. Seek out and talk with small growers near you. Gardening hobbyists may be eager to make a few dollars to support their habit by selling you dozens of peonies at the right time, branches of flowering crab apple, forced forsythia, or their prize German iris.

Throughout the seasons, nurseries that sell annuals, perennials, and flowering houseplants can be sources for unusual cut flowers. With proper conditioning, the materials you cut from nursery-grown plants will be fresh both botanically and conceptually. Tom Pritchard of Mädderlake, a marvelous flower and antique shop in New York City, is fond of using cuttings from azalea plants at Christmas time because the flowers hold up well, come in a range of shades from white to pale pink to deep red, and mix well with seasonal blooms.

Perennial herbs from the cutting garden are often still usable at Christmas. The scents of fresh rosemary, lavender foliage, and gray santolina in your arrangements raise your work above the ordinary.

CHILDREN'S CRAFTS

Children form a category all their own when it comes to lectures, demonstrations, tours, and workshops or articles and books about herbs and flowers. Your materials must be suitable to your audience, and the marketing process is different from that for adults. The income may be different also.

Many mothers who have attended my workshops have asked me to offer classes for children. In my checkered career, I have been a nature counselor at a day camp, a Girl Scout and Cub Scout leader, and had children of my own with whom to practice crafts activities. The work is not difficult, and it's exciting to watch the kids explore the world of flowers and herbs. Profit is another matter. Twice I offered workshops and found the attendance poor and the income worse, while the adult workshops were filled to overflowing. The expenses are the same for my time and for comparable materials, but parents are not willing to plunk down the same fee for their children as for themselves. Lowering the cost means increasing the number of students, leading to potential chaos. In addition, while adult students invariably make purchases after class, children rarely do. Those who most want to attend the classes are often involved in zillions of conflicting activities in their free time. Obviously, my marketing strategy hasn't worked, but maybe yours will. Consider offering flower parties in which you provide all of the activities, refreshments, and decorations. Please remember that, depending on the age, children are not usually venturesome in tasting new things and will groan over unusual flavors.

Each year I accept one or two invitations to present programs for local children's groups, which I do at no cost, as a contribution to my community. For business I stick to adults.

HOW TO FIND YOUR NICHE

You may prefer to be a generalist and include many directions in your planning. You can see, however, that each direction has its own professional literature and conferences, and each has its own opportunities for selling and promotion. Each will have its own wholesale sources that you will have to research. Buying well, at a good price, will help you to sell profitably. Concentrating in one niche may give you a better hook on which to hang the rest of your business. It's very hard to be a wedding specialist and also a corporate specialist, for example. In order to find out what works best for you in your area, brainstorm with a group of friends, preferably some who are knowledgeable about small businesses, for ideas that will fit your business needs and the market needs in your locale. Scout out the competition. Can a small town support two herb shops? Perhaps if you get a lot of tourist traffic or if you live in an upscale neighborhood or an active university town; other areas may not support it. How will your business be better or different? Brainstorm for other niches that you might fill within the flower and herb business. Can you specialize in books, millinery, or gifts with creative gift wrap?

Brainstorming involves listening to all ideas without evaluating or rejecting any. Sit down with your group, put a blackboard or flip pad on an easel in front of you, and start writing ideas as fast as they come. One person's idea will spark a suggestion from another. The ideas build on each other and may get fanciful, but don't stop until you are all completely dry. Now cross out ideas that are totally impractical or not to your liking. Discuss possibilities of other ideas and leave the best three to five to explore further.

In the flower and herb business, you are not purveying one of life's necessities. The feelings generated by your designs are usually more important than the objects themselves. In addition to the product, the customer is buying ambience. The customer's feelings are associated with you the artisan and your craft. Buying dried flowers at a department store or gift shop is an impersonal experience with little connection to the artisan. If you are a grower as well as a designer and selling retail, stress the country, farming, and ties to the land. Feeling connected to nature is a deep need many people experience. They crave the rural experience, even if they live in a city or town.

If you are a designer who buys her herbs and flowers, you may want to make the connection to a historical period or ethnic tradition. Witness the rapid growth of *Victoria* magazine, which emphasizes a return to romance and gracious living. The magazine started with a circulation of 435,139 in 1987 and by 1995 had a circulation of over 907,000.

Your display at a show or at your own shop, your logo, business cards, stationery, and all of your literature reflect the ambience you want to achieve.

I live in a small town 95 miles away from Philadelphia, 140 miles from New York, and 45 miles from Allentown, Pennsylvania. My barn attracts customers from those areas who want to take a drive to the country. I don't think it is because my work is more extraordinary than what they can get close to home, but the search is part of the thrill, and I try to capitalize on that by offering special teas and lunches for groups who want to make a day of it.

What special ambience do you have to offer? It may be your own personality, the type of product you specialize in, the collectibles you strew throughout your displays, or the teas and edibles you offer along with your decorative items. Barbara Pressler nestles her small perennial plant business, W. C. Fields, at the base of Hawk Mountain, a raptor sanctuary in Drehersville, Pennsylvania. Although most of her business is selling potted plants, she also offers some items each year that she crafts from found materials and "junque." Each is meant to decorate the garden. As customers wander through her whimsical landscape, they can view her unusual plants in a garden setting and look for the intriguing objects she offers for sale.

WHAT'S YOUR NAME?

As soon as you make the leap from hobby to business, the need for a name becomes apparent. What will you put on the top of your invoices? What will people call you, and in what name will you get credit approval from your suppliers? How will you advertise and seek publicity?

Your business name should fit your niche, your image, and your product; it should also be easy to spell, say, and remember. In starting a business, it seems impossible to project accurately where you will be in five years and what direction your business will take. But your name should allow for expansion.

When I sold my first dried flower and herb creations, I had no business name, but as soon as I felt the need I cooked a big family dinner. Over Kahlua cheesecake and coffee, we brainstormed. The names flew out thick and fast, one idea building on the next. I recorded each one and no longer remember which of the eight of us made the ultimate suggestion. The unanimous decision was The

Meadow Lark. I was still a full-time psychologist and working with flowers evenings and weekends. The business was a complete lark for me, and our meadow does support the habitat of the birds! Although the name sounded charming, I made two serious mistakes. In my small-town area, as a professional person for some years, my own name had instant recognition; my business name didn't. After ten years, local people still refer to my enterprise as "Ellen Platt's place," and when I advertise the business I find I must continue to put my own name in small letters so people make the connection. My second mistake was that the business name was too subtle. People passed my sign unaware that at the end of the long gravel drive they could find abundant flowers and herbs. The business name evolved from The Meadow Lark to Meadow Lark Flower & Herb Farm.

Any fictitious name like Floral Creations must be checked to see if someone else is using it. In my state at this writing, if your last name is not part of the business name, you must register your fictitious name in order to do business. For example, I could get away with Platt's Posies but not Ellen's Herb Corner. The phone company will not give you a business listing if you haven't registered your fictitious name.

Call your Department of State to check on the proper procedures and ask for an application. After you have returned it, the department will search its records for duplication and register the name as yours. Often you must pay a fee to register (currently $52 in Pennsylvania) and then advertise the name in a county newspaper and in a county law journal. An attorney can handle this matter for you, but you can also do it yourself. If you grow so big that you need to trademark a brand name, by all means get advice from an attorney.

QUALITY

Separate yourself from others who craft flowers and herbs by the quality of your workmanship. Your work must be as special as you can make it in both design and construction, regardless of the price. People who are perfectionists by nature will have no problem attending to details. School yourself to pay attention to particulars when making each arrangement.

Quality Transcends Price

A small pinecone ornament that has no blemishes, no broken pieces, no dribbles of glue, and unfrayed ribbon is a quality ornament if it also displays a freshness of style, even though it was made to sell at a modest price. Compare it with an expensive stacked arrangement that has some broken wheat, a few tipsy stems of larkspur, and an out-of-line rosebud; here the quality is poor.

What's New?

People come searching for what's new and different in design and material. If they came to your shop last month, they want to see something new this month. This year I added mountain mint, lemon mint, and anise hyssop to my herb garden, as well as the easy-to-grow but rarely seen lion's ear. People stop to ask for identification, and I provide them with information if they want to grow these herbs themselves.

No matter how extensive the selection, customers may still buy the same old baby's breath and eucalyptus. Some people far prefer the traditional in their homes, but they want to shop where new products are being introduced so that they can make the choice.

Service

Customers who prefer dealing with small stores rather than large, impersonal ones cite the service they receive as one of the factors. Your service should include the following:

1. Delivery when promised. This is an absolutely necessary but sometimes very difficult policy to follow because of seasonal fluctuations in the crafts business. You may be extremely busy before Christmas and Mother's Day; weddings might get out of hand. You may take too many orders at a show. Stay up nights; recruit your family; hire some temporary help—but deliver on time. Your future business depends on it.

If you promise delivery dates at a show and then ignore them, customers will complain about you to the management, and you will not be invited back. If you own a shop, word of mouth in your locality will label you as irresponsible, and customers will stay away in droves. If you know you can't deliver, be honest and give a realistic date. Often the customer will work with you, but if not, she is still a potential future buyer, rather than an enemy from the past.

2. Stand by your product. If for any reason the customer isn't satisfied, stand by your product. That doesn't require attaching a hangtag saying "money back guarantee," but it does mean acting in such a way that an adjustment is made easily, quickly, and cheer-

FREEZE-DRYING: A TECHNOLOGICAL NICHE, A TECHNOLOGICAL WARNING

When freeze-drying machines first came on the market not so long ago, a small one cost about $15,000. That meant you had to sell masses of freeze-dried materials to justify the initial cost. My retail shop couldn't justify the expense and I'm glad.

In the early days of technological wonder, the product was overhyped. Advertisements promised not only realistic shape and color, but flowers that would look the same forever. The industry had not, however, worked out the kinds of coatings that were necessary to spray over the flowers or dip them into to prevent reabsorption of humidity. Freeze-dried pink roses that I bought lost their color completely within six months, even faster than those dried in silica. Other flowers that I ordered, like gardenias, came sprayed with white paint, indicating that they had lost color in processing.

fully. Sometimes it may mean adding one or two flower stems in a place that looks sparse to the customer or changing the color of a bow. Especially with a custom-made design where the buyer doesn't see the finished product until she comes to pick it up, I want her to leave with a smile on her face. On the rare occasion that the requested changes are substantial, I detail a fee for increases in materials, and we agree on the changes in writing. I either make changes right then to save the customer an extra trip or deliver it later at no cost.

Once at a book signing my worst nightmare came true. I underestimated sales and ran out of books. To waiting buyers I offered to mail the book the next day, postpaid and, of course, with

When you hear of a new technology, you must decide whether to be one of the first to use it and corner the market or to wait and see if it will make financial and artistic sense for you.

Four years ago at a flower show, a shop owner visited me and waxed enthusiastic about the machine he had purchased. He was freeze-drying Queen Anne's lace, peonies, and a long list of garden flowers. I recently spoke to him again. He had stopped using the machine completely after a few months because he was unable to deal with the chemicals and fumes involved with post-treatment of the flowers. He sold the machine at a loss to someone else who wanted to try.

I still use freeze-dried materials to highlight some of my more expensive designs. I try to be realistic when touting these products. Compared with fresh flowers, the six- to twelve-month life span of freeze-dried flowers is good, but they don't have nearly the longevity of silk flowers. ❧

a personal inscription. Everyone accepted cheerfully. Take responsibility for your mistakes and try to rectify errors at no inconvenience or cost to the customer. Tell the customer you plan to avoid similar mistakes in the future.

3. The extras. Offer extra conveniences like UPS shipping, cartons for the customer to use herself, nearby delivery for large objects, or gift enclosures. Offer demonstrations and allow browsers to watch you work. Offer tips on the care of your wares and answer questions about the herbs and flowers you use or list them on hangtags on your product. Advertise custom work and offer to fill customers' own containers. Those family heirlooms, valuable antiques, or sentimental treasures are dear to the heart of your customer and will make your work even more appreciated, as well as saving the customer the cost of another basket she doesn't need. If you don't carry a product but know where the customer can find it, offer this information freely. Remember the old version of *Miracle on 34th Street* and how the customers flocked to Macy's after Santa Claus sent them to Gimbel's. Create loyal customers by offering information that they need.

✿ CHAPTER TWO ✿

Selling Retail

Selling wholesale and selling retail are business strategies with very different requirements. Few people successfully combine both strategies, and if you're just beginning a business, don't even think of trying to sell your crafts both ways. Read chapters 3 and 5 for a more complete description of each, along with pros and cons that will help you make up your mind.

Before you decide on your selling strategy, anticipate who will buy your product. Will it be a gallery, a gift shop, a furniture store, or a homeowner who wants to redecorate a room or enhance her decor? Are you selling mostly culinary herbs appropriate for gourmet shops and ultimately the kitchen? If your products are more bath-oriented, such as herbal oils, lip balms, and potpourris, think of the many fine bed and bath stores. Between the giftware building at 225 Fifth Avenue and the textile building at 295 Fifth Avenue in New York City, there are scores of showrooms displaying products for bed and bath buyers.

If your designs have a bridal flair, do you want to sell to bridal shops for weddings, showers, and gifts for the wedding party or would you prefer to sell directly to the bride and her party? Typically most of the dried flower and herbal products sold wholesale appear at gift and stationery trade (wholesale) shows and showrooms throughout the country. These shows attract buyers from all kinds of shops, from museum gift shops, bookstores, and specialty boutiques, to stationery and furniture stores. Or would you prefer to sell directly to the consumer? If you plan to sell retail, you need to determine who your buyers are likely to be.

WHO WILL BE YOUR CUSTOMERS?

Donna lives in Santa Fe, New Mexico, and wants to start a business selling dried flowers and herbs, some of which she grows herself. She anticipates marketing to the million or more tourists who flood the city each year and to the middle- to upper-income families who live there year-round and who, even if they love to garden and raise their own flowers, are constantly battling the problem of limited water resources. She is sure she can sell to those wealthy vacation home buyers who fly in for two months in opera season and for holiday weeks throughout the year, who would love to have a colorful, natural arrangement greet them each time they whirl in. Donna believes that her primary competition will come from fresh flower florists and from the colorful farmers' market at San Busco Center.

Lanie lives in Eugene, Oregon, and wants to start a business selling dried flowers and herbs, some of which she grows herself. She thinks a shop on Thirteenth Street will attract students from the University of Oregon for gifts to send to family and friends and for colorful room decorations. She expects to be particularly busy during parents' weekends and when the university hosts football games and track meets. She knows she must also have a following among the residents, many of whom teach or work at the university. She is aware that parking near the university is always a problem. She thinks her major competition for the student's gift and decorating dollar will come from the university bookstore. The competition for the resident's dollar will come from the many summer special events, like the arboretum shows where craftspeople sell their wares.

Sarah lives in Concord, New Hampshire, and wants to start a flower and herb business. Although Concord is the state capital, it is not one of the major New England tourist centers nor does it house a university. Sarah believes that, in addition to the middle- to upper-income homemaker, there is a large potential market in the professional offices and businesses that cluster in the capital. Her major competition will come from established florists, craft stores centered in town, and the summer and fall farmers' market.

Each of these women has tried to define her market in advance and, if correct, will have a strategy to start her marketing campaigns.

WHERE WILL YOU SELL?

Farm Stands

If you live in the country, you may be able to have a small stand on your property, even if only open one or two days a week on a regular basis to sell your wares. The key here is regularity and predictability, even if your days are few. With dried materials, weather is always a factor in display. Protecting your designs from sun, wind, and rain means that you must have a shelter that really shelters.

Zoning, parking, and public nuisance ordinances are issues to consider before trying your own stand. Regulations not only vary from locality to locality and street to street, but may also vary depending on whether you are considered a farmer (you grow the flowers and herbs yourself for your designs), a craftsperson who manufactures her product, or someone not crafting but buying for resale. Regulations are usually most favorable for farmers. Your county cooperative extension agent will have information about this. Suburban areas often have restrictions on home businesses that may not apply in rural or urban areas. Neighbors' complaints may lead to strict enforcement of certain regulations. Check it out before you go to the work and expense of creating a stand.

Some farmers in my area have unattended "honor stands." People buy produce and leave the money in a tin can. The farmer appears once in a while and collects the money. I tried this my first year in business, but my "honor stand" attracted some dishonorable people. Hire a teenager to watch your stand, if need be.

The Commonwealth of Pennsylvania publishes a brochure through the County Cooperative Extension Service listing all the farm stands, hours, and products throughout the state, with a map pinpointing the location of each. ᗒ **Ask if there is one put out by your state and get registered as a grower.** Once you are registered you should get a form in the mail each year before publication, enabling you to make any necessary changes. Newspapers throughout the state reproduce the map for their coverage area, so you get free publicity in two ways.

Market Stands

Farmers' markets, green markets, antique markets, flea markets, and fairs are highly popular with the locals and are often a tourist draw as well.

Vendors at farmers' markets usually pay booth rental fees and may be provided with tables or stands from which to sell. In some markets, like the Green Markets in New York City, which are open once or twice a week, farmers drive up in trucks and vans with their produce and set up their own awnings and tables, which they remove and cart home at the end of each day.

"Fresh from the farm" is a concept that attracts buyers, who trust that they will receive top quality at a reasonable price. The concept is so appealing to customers that some farmers' markets seek merely to fill their space and accept "farmers" whose crops are shipped in from Florida, California, or South America. They also may accept "farmers" of T-shirts and vanity license plates. Seek out markets that advertise "100% farmers" or "real farmers." Contact your County Cooperative Extension Office or your state Department of Agriculture to find out those locations and services that would be of most benefit to you and what your state has available to help farmers sell their produce.

My state currently offers the booklets *Starting and Strengthening Farmers' Markets in Pennsylvania* and *Farmers' Guide to Marketing*

Resources. They recently sent me a valuable fourteen-page publication entitled *Promoting Your Farmers' Market*.

You may not think of yourself as a farmer, but if you grow your own herbs and flowers, even in your suburban garden, it counts. With my one and a half acres under cultivation, I call myself a farmer when the benefits accrue to farmers. I am on the appropriate state mailing lists for all materials and courses on marketing what you grow. When I'm at garden writer conferences, I'm a writer. I think of myself as a teacher when I am giving workshops on dried flowers and herbs, and even when I am selling, because I want customers to understand what to expect from and how to treat their dried flower and herbal products, how to grow their own flowers, and how to dry them. I am still in my teacher frame of mind when I write, because I want you to benefit from what I know.

Adamstown, Pennsylvania, is known for its Sunday antique markets. Two large ones, mostly under roof, are open Sunday only, year-round, in an area where smaller stores and large co-ops abound. They are so well known that they are frequently written up in national publications. Though most of the stands sell genuine antiques or collectibles, there is one designer who has had a dried flower and herb stand for many years at the Black Angus Antiques Mart. Her arrangements are special, and people come year-round to find her there. Her prices are similar to those charged in fine stores and she does a fine business.

Flea markets range from low class to high class and are held periodically in many locales. The best are those that attract many antique and collectible dealers, not just those with overruns of T-shirts flaunting risqué sayings or boxer shorts in outlandish prints. As with the farm stands, weather is always a factor, so prepare for it. You'll do best if you are ready to make a commitment for the year. Customers will come back looking for you in the same spot, but ➣ **ask for a price concession from the promoter for doing several shows.**

Check out a county fair. It might be a wonderful place for your work. Look at the people who stroll the midway. Do they have packages in their hands or cotton candy? Are they clamoring around the craftspeople, waving their dollars, or are they dipping their french fries in ketchup and sauntering toward the music, a perfect way to have a cheap date? Make your own assessment before you pay the often hefty fee of renting a booth.

The Party Plan

Is there a homemaker alive in the United States who hasn't been to a home party given by a friend to sell makeup, giftware, clothing, jewelry, or Tupperware? Even if you have been successful against all odds in avoiding these events, you still know how they work. A party plan is a marketing strategy for retail sales. Instead of tying yourself down to the work and expense of a store, you set up shop in other people's homes. It provides a way of controlling your inventory because you take orders from samples before accumulating quantities of wares. Assume you make fifteen sample arrangements and offer each in two or three color combinations. If the one you predicted would be your hot item sells only two or three pieces, you haven't overstocked.

For your first party you find a willing friend or family member and encourage or bribe her to host a party for about thirty of her friends and coworkers. You provide the invitations and postage; she sends them out in her name. She provides light refreshments; you bring free gifts for all—a small favor like a sample of your potpourri. You provide a short program about flowers and herbs and a demonstration of your designs. People love to see arrangements being made and will ask questions about the materials and construction. You have order forms that the guests fill out; then you collect the money and provide a delivery date. The hostess delivers the goods to her invitees or they pick them up at her house. She gets 10 to 15 percent of the gross sales (less sales tax) in merchandise. For each party any of her guests book within the next thirty days, she receives a credit with a stated value toward your products, perhaps even a custom-made arrangement. Successful hostesses can both decorate their own homes and acquire gifts to give for all occasions throughout the year.

In order for this technique to grow into a viable business, you must be able to branch out into other friendship circles, neighborhoods, and towns. Your clientele will soon dry up if your hostesses have the same circle of friends.

The party-plan business grows by pyramiding the efforts. Hostesses who show promise in recruiting other hostesses can themselves become reps for you, now earning cash instead of merchandise. If they can become proficient at demonstrating and answering questions, they can put on their own parties with your samples. This is perhaps another story.

At each level, you must be sure that you can deliver the quantities of merchandise ordered and that you will continue to make a profit. You have control over the nature of the line and can change designs by giving out new sample products. Unlike plastic containers, flower and herb crafts deteriorate over time and with handling, and you must make provisions to refurbish or replace the samples, possibly after having a deep discount sale of the current samples.

Local Crafts Shows

Local crafts shows may range from the Christmas bazaar at the church down the street to juried shows sponsored by the volunteer committee of an internationally famous art museum. Some will not accept flower and herb crafts even of the finest quality, so check the rules before sending your work to be juried. See the discussion in chapter 5 on researching a wholesale show. The same techniques apply to retail shows. See what people are buying; notice which stands are busy. Check out the quality of the other stands.

Suppose your local library is having a crafts sale and is recruiting craftspeople to rent booths; the local business association is doing the same; and your own church or synagogue is having a fund-raiser and wants crafters to fill out a section of the children's carnival. The hospital auxiliary is staging a May fair and wants crafts booths lining the lawn. When deciding whether you should enter a show, approach it as a business decision, not a charity decision. If you want to donate to the cause, offer an arrangement for a raffle, send a wreath to the silent auction, or send a check for the coffers. Don't waste your time and belittle your work if the ambience isn't right for you. It will be much cheaper for you to stay home. You will avoid demeaning your product, and you won't waste a day out of your busy life.

On the other hand, you may judge that though sales will be sparse, the event is important enough that your being there has a strong public relations value. You may decide it's the perfect spot to hand out notices for your fall workshop schedule. You may choose to do the show to get your picture in the paper or to announce that you went to a show three states away even if you really went to see your best friend.

In turning down a local show, be gracious, express your regrets, offer to send a donation, say your schedule is full for the day (and then make sure it is) or say your policy is to only do shows after you've attended them once (an excellent policy to adhere to), but don't get dragged into an event that will not further your business goals.

Once you are established, you will receive invitations almost weekly to display and sell at crafts shows. Show organizers may want you, but do you want them? Will it be a profitable show for you? Is a show in the center of the mall really going to enhance your image as an artisan? If it's the right mall for you, maybe it will, but check it out first. In your pleasure at being invited, remember to do research first.

Bazaars and flea markets often look for crafters and may even offer free booth space as an incentive. But do you want your crafts to be seen with the crocheted pot holders and the fluffy refrigerator magnets?

Shows that charge an entry fee prequalify the audience as serious buyers; shows where people wander in free tend to attract crowds out for a pleasant stroll. It's certainly helpful to the show promoter to have you there with your special merchandise, and it's enjoyable for the crowds to see what you have done, but will it be enjoyable for you when you count your purse at the end of the day?

If turning down a show is hard, getting into a good show may be even harder. There is a waiting list, perhaps a long one. Don't be too easily discouraged. Craftspeople on waiting lists are not accepted strictly in order of application. Aside from any politics involved, each show promoter has criteria of her own. She is looking for the quality of your product and your display and diversity of the booths at the show. Customers will complain if booth after booth sells only eucalyptus wreaths. How boring!

For a large show in my area, the Kutztown Folk Festival, the promoter was looking for someone to replace the "pressed-flower lady," an elderly woman who had dropped out of the show after many years. I desperately wanted to get into that show but felt that I wouldn't sell enough pressed-flower designs to pay me to work for nine days in the grueling July heat in a six-by-eight-foot pigsty (the booth I was assigned on the fairgrounds houses hogs at the county fair). I negotiated with the promoter to sell my other herb and flower designs, like wreaths, arrangements, and even bunches of flowers, as well as pressed flowers.

The promoter may also have a theme in mind—a Victorian Mother's Day, a Day in the Country, an Old-Fashioned Christmas, or a particular ethnic tradition. If you can show how your product will fit into that theme, you are more likely to be chosen. When you research the show, look for vendors you know, even slightly. ∾ **Ask them to write to the promoter for you and check back to see that they have done so.** Send in photographs, write-ups about you from newspapers, and lists of other shows you have done.

Once you do a good show, it is much easier to keep upgrading your shows till you reach the top.

State Crafts Guilds

Most of the state craftsmen's guilds and the American Craft Council exclude floral designers from their shows, and thus we miss outstanding outlets for our wares. But the local chapters of craftsmen's guilds in the counties are often more welcoming and will accept floral designers as members, perhaps only if they grow their own materials. Usually other members must recommend a new person. Determine whom you know in the guild and ∾ **ask her to look at your work and to recommend you.** The advantages of joining are many. You must be juried to get in. That means you must show slides or show your actual work, usually five examples. The work must be original, well conceived, and well executed. An impartial group will eye your work in a professional way; no longer will it be just your friends telling you how wonderful you are!

If you aren't accepted, the jury may write comments about your work, which should be highly informative. You can try again after a brief period of time; try to change those elements that the jury rated down.

When you are a member, your creative juices will be stimulated by all the other members, by the meetings in which outside artists present their work, and by the need to stay on your toes. During guild shows there may be an on going jurying process, whereby a committee of some of the most respected members walk the floor in a group and may ask craftspeople to remove certain items if they're not up to standard.

The local guilds sponsor retail crafts shows, usually one or two a year, the most important being a Christmas show. The show by definition is nonprofit and close to home, so your expenses will be low. Customers who come through the show will be mostly local too, so they are a wonderful source of names for your mailing list. Even those who don't buy from you at the show may keep your card and buy from you on another occasion.

Flower Shows
It takes experimentation to find the most successful shows for your work. Flower shows have always been better than mixed media crafts shows for my business. At a mixed media show, visitors come with quilts on the brain or jewelry in their hearts. They hope to find the perfect pillow for the guest room, a teapot for their embryonic

collection, a creative toy for the new grandchild, and, yes, they also come for flowers. But at a flower and garden show the primary focus is narrowed. Of course, growers of potted orchids and African violets, the bulb specialists, and the seed vendors all vie with you for the consumer's dollar, but the focus is on things that grow.

For me the top is the Philadelphia Flower Show, the largest indoor flower show in the world, and many think the best, comparing it favorably to the famous Chelsea Flower Show in England. It attracts more than 225,000 people in nine days. Sponsored and produced by the Pennsylvania Horticultural Society, it is a massive fund-raising effort for their Philadelphia Green project, which helps city neighborhoods develop community gardens.

The show is a major tourist attraction; people fly in from around the country and even from around the world, and almost no one leaves the show without buying something. The show is notorious among vendors for the length of its waiting list. Here's my story.

During my second year in the dried flower and herb business, I turned to a free state tourist publication promoting all the fairs and festivals in Pennsylvania. It listed dates and phone numbers for information. Looking through the guide, I checked all the events that seemed possible for me and started making calls. I got more information on prices, requirements for vendors, and the state of the waiting list. One of my choices was the Fall Harvest Show sponsored by the Pennsylvania Horticultural Society. A small, homey show in the Horticultural Center of Fairmount Park, it was just the right size, price, and length (Friday evening, Saturday, and Sunday). I had a free place to stay, could pack everything in my van and drive the ninety-five miles easily, and had family helpers volunteering their services in the city. The first show was a sales success, and my booth received many compliments. The woman in charge of vendors at this low-key Harvest Show was also in charge of vendors at the Philadelphia Flower Show, and we spent some time schmoozing about that grand show. I was vaguely interested but didn't feel ready for the challenge. When she asked me if I'd like to get on the waiting list, I said yes because I had heard the list was about five years long. I figured by then I'd be ready.

That same January, I got the fateful call. There was a last-minute drop-out in the grand flower show, and I was offered the booth. I had three days to decide before the next vendor would be contacted.

When we need advice we often turn to the person who will tell us what we want to hear. I called my daughter. Not only did she offer to drive down from New Hampshire to help set up, but my son-in-law offered to design and construct the booth and bring it with them. My son and daughter-in-law offered to help pack up for the return trip. My children pushed me over the precipice. I accepted the space I was assigned. After one more year I started badgering for a bigger booth in a better location. After two more years I was able to move to prime real estate, a twelve-by-twenty-foot booth with three open sides. People found me just as they left the garden display floor and entered the Marketplace. The show was recently moved to the new convention center in Philadelphia. Because I am a longtime vendor with several ribbons earned for booth display, I was granted with first choice of spaces. The moral is this: Always be ready to take an acceptable risk.

In doing a show, it may take three years to build up your word-of-mouth business. Satisfied customers return for repeat business; lookers of one year return to buy another year. The good news and the bad news is when a customer stops by to tell me that her purchase from a previous year still looks so fresh that she doesn't need anything else.

In a large show it is extremely helpful to remain in the same locality. Move your booth at your peril; move only to get an obvious upgrade in space or location. Don't move for frivolous reasons, and don't move every year.

Adopt the policy of sending reminder cards to customers who live in the area of the show inviting them to come and see your new designs. If possible, add a personal note or signature to bring in business. Especially when you have moved your location, send a card with your new booth address.

MOVING UP

As soon as you sell at a show of some size, promoters will find you. They come from far and wide to shop for new craftspeople. They have to fill their convention centers, field houses, armories, civic centers, and ballrooms with a diversity of classy craftspeople with

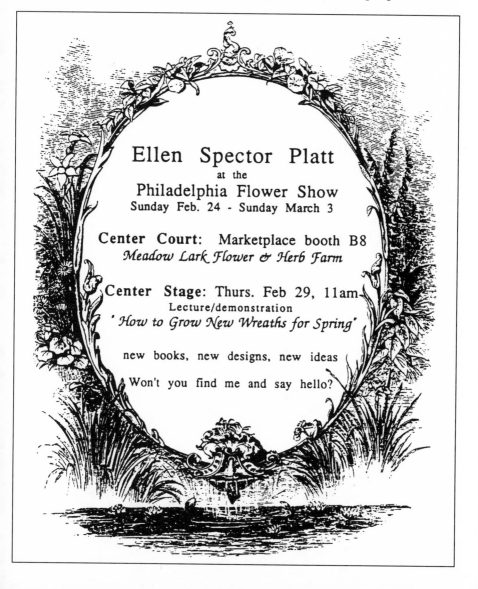

Ellen Spector Platt
at the
Philadelphia Flower Show
Sunday Feb. 24 - Sunday March 3

Center Court: Marketplace booth B8
Meadow Lark Flower & Herb Farm

Center Stage: Thurs. Feb 29, 11am
Lecture/demonstration
'How to Grow New Wreaths for Spring'

new books, new designs, new ideas

Won't you find me and say hello?

creative displays and new-looking products. They are looking for you, and they need you as much as you need them.

At the Philadelphia Flower Show I have been invited to appear in San Francisco, Boston, New York, St. Louis, Cleveland, Rhode Island, and Chelsea-America, as well as myriad smaller shows. I've been approached by representatives from garden clubs looking for speakers, botanical gardens looking for places to tour, and the usual assortment of benefit and fund-raiser chairpersons looking for booth holders. One of my favorite invitations was to a decorators' show house to benefit a cancer charity in Margate, New Jersey, the Show House at the Shore, where I was invited to present a program on decorating with flowers.

My rule for seeing a show before doing it doesn't apply when management is paying me a fee for speaking, rather than my paying them a fee for renting booth space. I only wish I had asked to see the place where they were putting me up for the night, because the room donated by an Atlantic City casino was the most garish, gaudy, noisy, and generally tawdry place I had ever seen. On my return to the Show House at the Shore, the hosts were kind enough to accede to my request for a room more befitting this flower farmer.

CHAPTER THREE

The Retail Show Circuit

Crafters in all media can make a living traveling from show to show, without any permanent retail space of their own. It is an arduous life, involving packing and unpacking both before and after each show, hauling, carting, setting up a booth and taking it down again, traveling and being away from home on a regular basis. As draining as they can be, shows can also be profitable in themselves and lead to other opportunities. Every craftsperson I know has done some selling at shows, often as a way of getting started with minimal investment of money or time. You can control the number of shows you do a year and schedule appearances around family life or a full- or part-time job.

BEFORE THE SHOW
Choose a noteworthy show and check on the look of the show, the attendance figures, and the demographics. Try to predict what this audience will buy. For example, I know that to garden club members I will sell lots of flowers and herb bunches, some containers and books, but almost no finished arrangements. Most members are skilled at designing their own and enjoy the challenge.

Gather all the literature, do some research, and decide whether it is to your advantage to do a particular show. Much of my decision is based on how high the expenses will be, including show fees and expenses for overnights and travel. Shipping charges for a booth and merchandise plus travel and hotel expenses can make selling retail prohibitive. From Pennsylvania, San Francisco is too expensive but New York is an acceptable three-hour ride. With a rental truck, a free place to stay, and friends to help, I can do a potentially profitable show. In addition, New York is a market where magazine editors and publishers often appear. It is close enough to home that some visitors to the show may drive to the country to see my barn and farm, a benefit that is lost if shows are out of a day's driving range.

Obtain information from the promoter about the drawing area of the show and how long it has been in business at that locale. ᕦ **Ask where your booth location will be and make certain that it will be under cover and not exposed to the elements. Ask whether uniform signs for the booths, tables, and coverings are provided and whether you are required to use them.** Consider all your expenses. Ask whether you and your helper get free parking passes or a reduced rate. Find out if you must pay extra for electricity and if there is an outlet near your booth. I require one because I go *nowhere* without my hot glue gun.

You may be invited to rent a booth at a show and wind up giving a program instead. The Pittsburgh Home and Garden Show promoters once approached me to rent a booth. I had never seen the show. It was too far away for a one-day drive to look. Since they were eager to attract more flower people, and I was eager to promote my first book, I asked if they would like a demonstration instead, and we came to financial terms for my appearance. The show turned out to be primarily a retail home show, with lots of replacement windows and home spas for sale. But the promoters had hired a super ad agency that placed feature articles about me in three newspapers and landed me an invitation to appear on a two-hour Sunday-morning gardening show. As a promotional venture, it was an excellent use of my weekend. If I had contracted for a booth there to sell my dried flower and herb designs, I know I would have died.

How Much to Take

One of the hardest parts of doing a retail show is determining how much of your product to take. As when cooking for a dinner party, you want to make more than enough so that some is left when the last person is served. If you run out completely you are wasting an opportunity to sell, and the booth looks sad with only a few remaining items. If you take too much you have the chores of packing up, transporting, and unpacking at home, with all the attendant breakage problems. With seasonal items, like Christmas arrangements, you may not have another sales opportunity till next year. By then your beautiful arrangements may be headed for the compost heap.

One technique for figuring how much to take is to start with how much you need to earn and work backward.

Start by estimating your expenses. Your show space costs $550 for a small but elegant two-day show. Electricity is provided. You are borrowing a van, but gas and parking will cost $25. You're paying a local helper $150. The motel costs $75 including tax. Meals are mostly brown bag and inexpensive, but restaurants will add $35. Total out-of-pocket expenses will be $810. If you sell $810 retail value of crafts, you are losing money, not breaking even, because you are not counting the cost of the goods and the cost of your selling time.

For the moment assume a 300 percent markup of goods. That is, if your materials and time cost $20, you sell the arrangement for $60. Just to break even you will need to sell $1,215 worth of goods to pay your show expenses of $810. (The cost of goods is one-third of $1,215, or $405. The rest of gross goes to pay direct show expenses of $810.) How much do you hope to sell at the show to come home happy? If you take only $1,200 worth of goods, you are sunk before you even start, because even if customers pick you clean you will lose money by doing this show. Take enough to sell to make a nice profit and still have some wares left over to keep your display interesting till the show ends. Naturally there is no guarantee that you will sell the projected amount even if you are fully prepared, but if you don't have the merchandise with you, you're guaranteed not to sell it.

Diversify but Don't Clutter

The starting point of most novices going to a show is panic: "I'd better make this style, and maybe nobody will want it, so I'd better make another style just to be sure." Such thinking can run rampant and lead you to an infinite number of designs. Your booth space is certain to be small, perhaps eight by twelve feet or at the most ten by twenty feet.

Your designs may be lovely, but if everything is jumbled together, it's hard for customers to shop at your booth and make up their minds. Resist the temptation to make too many different kinds of things. Instead, make a master plan of colors and designs that will pull your look together. You should achieve a balance between cluttering your booth with dozens of different types of products, each in a different color and design, and selling only blue topiaries; seek variety but not chaos.

Storage

Be prepared to take custom orders at a retail show if you are willing to ship. Most shoppers, however, are eager to go home with their treasures, and you should plan to accommodate them. Since flower and herb vendors generally offer bulky merchandise (compared with jewelry vendors, for example), plan on some storage for your wares. Your van is a relatively inconvenient spot for additional merchandise because it will probably be parked some distance from your booth, and you are sure to need something at the busiest time of the day. ᖇ **Ask the show promoter if there is a locked storage room and make a reservation to use it.**

The New York Flower Show used to be one of the worst venues for storage. When I first did that ten-day show and trucked my cartons of flowers and crafts from home to the pier where the show was held, the only place to stash them was outside on a long walkway running the length of the pier that was closed to the public. Vendors would label their cartons and tie them with tarps to keep out the weather, hoping that they wouldn't get stolen. My inaugural year at the show opened to a winter storm, a blizzard with strong winds howling. The pier workers decided to move all the cartons to an unlocked storage room at the end of the pier. Fortunately for us all there were no losses that year—probably the weather was too bad for vandals and thieves.

Restock your booth each day before the show opens, or after hours if you still have the strength (I never do). Design your booth to house extra merchandise either under the display tables or behind your backdrop.

Vendors who live near a show have an advantage because they can get daily deliveries from their workshops or bring more merchandise each day themselves. For a long show that's farther away, you can arrange with a helper at home to ship more merchandise by UPS; plan ahead what the delivery schedule will be and keep in contact with your helper regarding which things are selling best and what kind of stock you need.

Price Range

Craftspeople find it helpful to have a line of small items, under $15, for those who are looking for something to take home from the show without making a dent in the budget.

Design one or two "show-off" pieces, the top of your price range, which you bring specifically to elicit oohs and aahs from show visitors and media reporters. Display them in a prominent spot and let them enhance your display. You may sell them; I often do, but don't expect to. Their purpose is to show off what your skill can accomplish if money is no object, create excitement, and raise the perceived attractiveness of your lesser-priced wares.

Think of a fashion designer who designs suits and dresses selling for thousands of dollars, affordable to only a select few. He licenses his name and then produces silk scarves, belts, or costume jewelry, which many more shoppers can afford and are eager to have. They just seem to look better than similar scarves by another manufacturer without the name. Try to develop your own name by letting the world know how talented you are.

Your regular line of crafts will sell at a variety of prices between your pick-up items and your show-off pieces. Imagine a price pyramid. More of your flower and herb crafts will sell in the low to mid range. In terms of quantity, fewer will sell as you get to the peak in price. (See chapter 10 for a discussion of how to price your wares.)

AT THE SHOW

Show off the wares in your display. Feature your best work effectively in a booth or stand that has a professional touch. Whether you construct the booth yourself or have it made for you, it should be flexible enough to fit in different size spaces. If you do several shows a year, the odds are that the space requirements for your booth will be slightly different among shows.

The materials and colors you select should serve as a fitting background to the style of your work and show it up effectively. Quality here means freshly painted, unwrinkled, unchipped (unless you are deliberately selecting a primitive style) and artfully decorated in a way that doesn't detract from your craft. The decoration will vary with the season and perhaps with the setting.

The year I took some antique keepsake containers to a show to hold my bunches, I had offers for the antiques, which I had to reject. Those were the times that I wished I were in the antique business. Now I take less-conspicuous containers or those that I am willing to part with for a price.

Lighting

There is one truism of all shows, wholesale and retail: *Whatever lighting is provided is never adequate.* ∿ **Ask what outlets, extension cords, and alternative lighting are available.** Arrange for rentals (expensive) or for auxiliary spots you bring yourself. Plan your lighting to highlight your most important work.

Signs and Labels

Price tags should be legible and uniform; your booth sign should be professionally done, not homemade looking. Computers are excellent for professional-looking designs. If you can't do it yourself, go to one of the many shops that will give a quick turnaround time.

Hangtags on your wares can be used to write the prices and give information about the product. They include your well-designed logo, name, and phone number, and add a nice touch to your work.

Assigning names to certain designs helps sales. Meg Southerland of Gardenworks in Salem, New York, sells her crafts at her parents' raspberry farm. Among her many lovely pieces, she designed a line of wreaths made out of raspberry canes and labeled them Razzmatazz. What a perfect name to attract attention and inform the customer.

I found closed bamboo boxes with domed lids and designed miniature gardens inside. They were admired, but few sold until I put a sign with them calling them Secret Gardens. Then they started flying away.

Hanging a twig design on the wall for display gives people the immediate impression of how they could use it in their home; displaying it on a table isn't so obvious until you call the same twig design a Table Topper. You can almost see the light bulb flashing on as people say, "That would make a wonderful centerpiece in my dining room."

Dressing the Part

You and any helpers at the show should dress the part, enhancing the booth display. My elegant friend Kim Ost, a jewelry designer, dresses up and models her jewelry at every show—silver bangles up and down her arms, silver beads at her neckline. I can't imagine a more perfect way to display her crafts.

The theme of the show can set the tone of your dress. A show in a historic home requires different outfits than does a stand at a flea market. At spring shows my helpers and I all wear the beribboned straw hats we trim with flowers and herbs and offer for sale.

Helpers enjoy the association with the booth as they get a chance to walk around the show. We've sold many a hat during a lunch break, as we model while we eat our picnic.

Whether it's special colors that highlight your merchandise or T-shirts or aprons with the name of your business, a uniform look enhances what you sell.

Display in Your Booth

Many of the same rules apply here that apply to a shop (see chapter 4). Small vignettes of related merchandise attract attention and are easy for the shopper to understand. Pressed-flower note cards are displayed with pressed-flower mats and pictures in antique frames. Battenburg lace angels holding dried flower bouquets are grouped with pristine linen-covered vases on a high stacker. Within each grouping, there is a price range of merchandise. Wreaths and arrangements for office decor and less feminine designs may be grouped together; another area might display seasonal arrangements, such as those with fall harvest, Halloween, and Thanksgiving themes with burnt orange, scarlet, and gold dried fruits and berries.

In each booth there seems to be a spot of honor, and whatever you place there immediately attracts attention and sells. It will vary from setting to setting, depending on the traffic pattern of the show, your display layout, and lighting. Take notice of where this spot is. You may want to move a few items later in the day so that you will sell the things you most want to.

If you're selling nosegays or mixed bunches of flowers and herbs, you may want to leave one out to be touched, smelled, felt (and ruined), and the others prewrapped in cellophane for instant pickup and protection. (When pricing your items, remember to include the cost of the cellophane.) Items like the white Battenburg lace angels mentioned above should be kept safe in Lucite boxes or hung far out of reach of grimy fingers .

At shows where people are constantly touching and handling your wares, put the tough stuff in the front where rough handling may occur. Or arrange your display so that it can't be handled, pinned to backgrounds or placed in covered cases.

In my barn, where most of my dried flowers are displayed by hanging, there is little problem from handling. At my first flower show, however, I stuffed large baskets with colorful dried flowers to sell by the bunch and set the baskets at different levels at the most conspicuous corner of the booth. The display was eye-catching; people clustered and grabbed. I was left with a large quantity of instant potpourri. Now I have bins stacked eight feet tall in the back of my booth. Flowers and herbs are laid in the bins, heads pointing out, forming a glorious quilt of color. Only my hands and those of my helper touch the materials until the time of the sale. At the front of my booth I put pressed-flower note cards packed in cellophane, baskets and unbreakable containers, potpourris, and small, sturdy arrangements.

Those crafters happiest with their booths seem to be the ones who have opted for a design that is easy to transport, carry, set up and take down, and doesn't blow over in the wind or leak in the rain. Elements that stack, fold, nest, or come apart without hardware are favorites. Since the older you get the heavier your booth seems to get, portability can be a prime requisite.

ATTRACTING A CROWD

Even if your booth is an eye-catcher and your craftwork is magnificent, there will still be times when you wonder where all the customers have gone. You must *always* look alert, interested, pleasant, and welcoming, even if at the end of a show you are ready to bat the next person who fingers the larkspur and asks if it's real. Reading is forbidden, even if your book is far more engrossing than the crowd. Gossiping with your helper turns attention away from potential business, even if her story is more enchanting than your sales.

An ideal way to attract a crowd is to demonstrate your craft. Clear a tiny space where people can see you and start making bows, designing a new arrangement to replace one you just sold, or working on a wall hanging that doesn't demand too much concentration. As soon as the first person comes to watch, start narrating to her as you work. "I'm using about two yards of ribbon to make this bow and the ribbon is wired down both sides, making it very easy. Did you ever use ribbon like this? It makes an expert out of a novice. . . ." Some people seem to need permission to ask you a question, and your narration indicates your willingness to talk.

The object is not really to churn out the production here, but to use your slack time in a way that will maintain the interest of both you and your potential customer. One person standing raptly in front of your both always attracts another; then everyone must come and see what's so interesting. And if you get a few more items made, you're using your time most productively. Be ready to switch gears from making to selling. Continue to welcome each person to the booth, never losing sight of the primary reason that you are there—to sell.

In preparing for each show, I plan which type of craft I will demonstrate and bring along a convenient box of the "fixings" to take out when the need arises. Don't follow my example and take out your pressed-flower materials to demonstrate at an outdoor show on a windy day. Picture about a dozen show visitors scattering in the grass, trying to retrieve pressed buttercups and pansies. Well, I did attract attention!

SHOW SUPPLIES CHECKLIST
In addition to your booth construction (tables, shelves, and so forth) and your merchandise, come prepared for most eventualities. Here is my permanent checklist that I adapt to the needs of each show:

Display
    stool
    stepladder for setting up
    hand truck or dolly
    special display racks for hats, books, and note cards
    reachers (for high places)

extra lights
heavy-duty extension cords and outlet strip
flame-retardant table covers
mirrors (for customers trying on hats)
covers for night protection, tarps for rain protection
    (even some indoor sites leak)

Office Supplies

sales slips
cash box with lots of change
business cards, brochures, press kit, special literature
two calculators
bags
tissue paper or cellophane wrap
stapler
paper clips and rubber bands
cellophane tape
sealing tape for cartons at end of show
extra price tags and hangtags
sign
clipboard with attached pen and mailing list sign-up sheet
extra pens and pencils
credit card machine and forms
envelope with show contract, insurance certificate,
    and related papers
sales figures from previous year's show

Floral Supplies

extra moss, foam, floral prongs, and stickum
lazy susan (for demonstrating arrangements during the show)
hot glue gun and glue sticks (plus an extra in case gun breaks
    down during a demo)
clippers and scissors
extra materials for demonstrating

Tools

broom, whisk, and dustpan
clips or hooks for hanging
extra wire for hanging
hammer and screwdriver
assorted nails and screws
water mister for some flowers

Personal

thermos
small cooler
overnight clothing and a warm vest
tote bag
secret money holder
work aprons with logo
aspirin and Band-Aids

BEYOND SELLING

Your main goal is probably to sell your lovely crafts and make a profit. Don't waste your valuable time and money. A show is a splendid opportunity to achieve many other goals. Plan to accomplish *at least* three more goals at each show. State these goals in advance and prepare the necessary steps to achieve them. Here are a few suggestions:

1. Give out your card telling people where and how to reach you for future orders. Include a small map if your business location is hard to find. If you have your cards out for the taking, bring a huge quantity, as there are literature gleaners who aren't happy unless they take home a shopping bag full of paper goods.

2. Collect names and addresses of *interested* people, including all paying customers, for your mailing list. Postage is far too expensive to collect names indiscriminately. To collect only those names of people with a genuine interest, I don't leave my clipboard in plain sight. I offer it gladly to anyone who asks. I also tell my

helpers to ask any person who asks us questions but doesn't buy, "Would you like to be on our mailing list?"

3. Distribute literature for your next open house, series of classes, or major event.

4. Have a special card listing your other regular services, such asspeaking to groups, programs for garden clubs, tours of your garden, or afternoon teas. Include your name, address, phone number, and directions, but not prices, as these may become obsolete before your print run is exhausted.

5. Find out from show management what media representatives are visiting the show. Make a strong effort to talk to one of them.

6. Walk the show floor to see what the immediate competition is like and what their prices are. Establish a friendly rapport with your competition. You can often help each other as you share common problems. Don't ask for sales figures, because they probably won't tell you the truth anyway, but if they've been there before and you haven't, ask how this year's show compares with other years.

7. Gain inspiration from the creativity of other designers. Looking at the stunning creations of other artisans, whether in your particular field of flowers and herbs or another medium like pottery, paper, wood, or glass, broadens your own outlook.

At a flower show, take the time to see the work of the competitive classes. Many entrants are labeled amateurs because they don't make their living with flowers, but their designs are as artistic as many professionals and far more artistic than some.

8. Make it easy to receive other invitations. Promoters and organizers for other shows and events will be at the show looking for the best craftspeople to invite to their shows. If someone approaches you, however, don't make a decision on the spot. Think about it for a week or so, and see how that event fits in with your goals and with your schedule.

My first year at the Philadelphia Flower Show, the tour organizer for the Brooklyn Botanic Garden stopped by and, admiring my merchandise, asked about bringing a tour to my farm. Without thinking, I told her I didn't feel my small farm was suitable as the destination for a day-long outing from Brooklyn. I neglected to get her card. How I wish she had returned the next year.

I now have people and places to tap for a glorious day in the country: Barbara Pressler's garden gem, W. C. Fields, where she sells rare and unusual perennials; internationally famous Hawk Mountain bird sanctuary; Ruth Flounder's Sculps Hill Herb Farm; and several restaurants and farms that are delighted to welcome groups of out-of-town guests.

Have your card or literature ready to hand to those who inquire, and ask for their card or literature in return. Always offer to call back to discuss the event within the next two weeks. Be ready with names and phone numbers of other nearby places of interest to round out the day.

EXPENSES
Booth rental fees, and often electricity fees, are inevitable at a show, but other expenses mount up to make the difference between profit and loss. Consider the following ways of saving money.

Find Low-Cost Help
Do you need to pay a helper to go with you? Especially for your first few shows, if they run only one or two days, a close friend or family member may be eager to help you for the fun of it. Can you trade labor by helping your friend with some other chore at a later date? Offer a day's work in her garden or help with decorating for Christmas or a special party.

Once you know you will be on the regular show circuit, paid help may be essential, but try other options at the beginning. I got some wonderful experience at shows before starting my flower and herb business by helping a close friend who is an antique dealer. Many of the issues of selling at antique shows are similar to crafts shows, and I learned from my friend the important ritual of making excuses for poor attendance or poor sales at shows to buoy confidence. It's too hot; its too cold; its too sunny, and everyone is out golfing or swimming; it's too snowy, and everyone is skiing; it's too rainy for people to go out; if only it would rain there would be nothing else for people to do but come here; the show wasn't promoted well; the show was promoted so well it's too crowded for people to buy—you get the idea.

Save on Overnight Expenses

At the beginning of your career, choose to do shows where you can return home at night or have a friend to stay with. Stay at inexpensive motels. This is work, not a vacation. Crafters with campers often stay overnight on the show grounds if in a safe locality.

Bring Your Own Sustenance

Meals at shows are notoriously expensive. What are your alternatives? With convenience shops and salad bars, breakfast and lunch are easy to pick up on the way to a show. The show caterer is there to make money, often with a gourmet feast. Many crafters appear with meals packed in coolers and big insulated jugs of ice water. (Talking to hundreds of people is a thirsty occupation.) Where there are outlets, I've seen people with their own hot pots for instant soup, tea, or coffee. My practice at the Philadelphia Flower Show is to buy a cup of tea each morning, keep the foam cup, bring my own tea bags and lemon, and ask for refills of hot water only. Tea drinker that I am, I save at least $55 on tea alone for the eleven days of setup and show time. I pay for the one cup a day to try to be fair to the food service operator who supplies me with the courtesy of hot water. Other places are not so generous. I have been turned down for hot water in New York on many occasions.

GETTING OUT OF SHOW BIZ

If you exhibit at shows when you begin your business, you know how hard it is: packing, unpacking, setting up, selling, and then the reverse trip of packing all that you didn't sell and unpacking at home. A lot of labor is involved beyond the actual time at the show, and invariably there is some damage in transportation.

Some artisans go on a regular show circuit; it is the major way of retailing their wares. Merle Walker, the former executive director of the New Hampshire League of Craftsmen and now an arts consultant, feels that every artisan's goal should be to get out of the show business within five years. At the very least, after a period of experimentation, your knowledge of which are your best shows and which you can dump will make the selling life more profitable and more enjoyable. I know that I will never again sell from a pigsty in the July heat.

That means that while you are doing shows, you must plan for the future. If you are selling wholesale, you should have a cadre of customers who will continue to buy from you and a long mailing list of other potential customers to whom you can mail your brochures. You may have reps who sell your work at shops around the country. If you are making crafts that sell at a high price, like furniture, you may have regular galleries that represent you.

If you are selling retail, you may have your own shop and vow never to travel again.

❧ CHAPTER FOUR ❧

The Retail Store

M any artisans who choose the route of retail merchandising progress slowly toward owning their own stores. They start selling to friends and coworkers, then at crafts and flower shows or home parties, and perhaps submitting a few pieces to stores on consignment. They gain confidence in their own abilities, both in design and in business. They make many mistakes along the way and learn to solve problems. They work out profitable pricing schemes and study the markets. They set aside profits earmarked to invest in their dreams. All the while they may be working at other full- or part-time jobs, or watching toddlers become school-age children, freeing up some time.

If your dream is to own a retail store featuring your own flower and herb crafts, here are some considerations.

WHAT PRODUCT WILL YOU SELL?
When you went to several shows a year, you geared up for each in a whirlwind of creative activity and replenished your stock in between. To have the type of selection that can hold the attention of browsers, a store requires plentiful stock at the outset. Soon you

will discover that it is almost impossible for one person to create all the merchandise for stock and wait on customers whenever the store is open. If you are also trying to grow your own flowers and herbs, delete the *almost* from the previous sentence. It is impossible.

When I first started in business I ordered a small supply of interesting tins, baskets, and glassware to hold the arrangements I was constructing. Since my workshop is part of my retail space, customers who came in to browse among my flowers often asked to buy one of the containers. At first I was too naive to listen to my customers; I politely said, "No, that is part of my supply pile." It took five such requests before I stuck price tags on all the containers and ordered enough to both serve my own needs and allow for plenty of merchandise to sell.

When I noticed that browsers were picking up and reading the flower and herb books from my personal reference shelf, I quickly added a stock of books for sale. Each new item I ordered increased the potential value of a sale. Someone came in to buy a few bunches of flowers and left with a container, some floral foam, and a vial of essential oil to scent the finished piece. In sales, the add-ons can make the difference between profit and loss.

Especially at the start, keep the image of your store carefully in mind, and don't stray far from the track. If yours is a gallery-type shop, keep everything handmade, though not necessarily by you. This way you can play up that image in all your promotions. You can highlight other crafters, their backgrounds, and personal stories. If yours is a crafts-type shop where you are featuring the dried flowers and herbs you raise and are selling bunches along with your finished designs, consider selling craft supplies as well, such as foam, wire, glue guns, interesting containers, and books that give instructions.

WHAT AMBIENCE AND IMAGE WILL YOU SELL?
Depending on where you live, who you are, your design preferences, and where your store will be, create a cohesive image for your shop from the beginning. Many of your other decisions will

become easier once you decide on your "look." If you already own some space that you plan to convert into a shop, the type of space often dictates your image.

I live on the outskirts of a small town that has no tourist industry or university draw. Local farms are being sold off and developed for housing and small commercial ventures. Our own five acres were purchased from a developer who built town houses and single-family homes on either side of the old stone farmhouse and barn. But we made a little island amid the building lots, and part of what was a sprawling farm since the mid-1800s continues as a tiny flower and herb farm. The ambience is dictated by the fact that I wanted from the start to grow and dry my own flowers. Selling was initially a means to enable me to support my compulsion to grow more flowers.

Because my barn houses the shop, my customers enter an area where the flowers are drying and are also for sale. Those who can't wait for a newly harvested crop to become completely dry will often snag a bunch from the drying line to hang at home in a warm, dry spot, thus entering into the process with me. Before you start to worry that your space is not comparable, remember that the down side of a barn is that it is difficult to heat (we don't even try and must close all winter) and to control the humidity in summer without great expense.

I've seen other structures that are finished in a barnlike manner, where purchased flowers and herbs hang down from the ceilings and the rural atmosphere is re-created. One of my favorite shops used to be on the main street of Woodstock, Vermont. In a town where the zoning regulations are exceedingly strict, the shop gained atmosphere from its neighboring white clapboard, dark-shuttered colonial buildings. The small shop was just steps from the famous Woodstock Inn. Even when the snow was piled shoulder high at the curbs, visitors could walk across the street to see and purchase the creative designs of the owner. A shop surrounded by this atmosphere needs a good proportion of traditional designs to please visitors to the town seeking an authentic colonial experience.

Another favorite, which couldn't be more different, is on Route 84, sixty miles from Santa Fe, New Mexico. To an easterner who drives through the arid hills to get to the shop, it feels just like the West of legend and is, in fact, in the middle of the Sangre de Cristo Mountains. If you speak to the delightful owner, Loretta Valdez, she will discuss the corn, peppers, gourds, and other materials her family grows on the farm behind her shop, her designs and her ambience intricately interwoven.

A warning: While proprietors often feel that the theme of the store is crucial, surveys of customers list cleanliness at or near the top of the list of reasons why they like a store. Pay particular attention if you are selling medicinal or culinary herbs. Note too that dried flowers and herbs can drop their petals with continual handling. A customer often doesn't realize that she is the twenty-ninth person to pick up a basket of flowers for a closer look, fondling them to see if they're real, and doesn't comprehend the damage she causes by so doing. Make sure that you and your sales staff keep the counters well whisked and the floors frequently swept of customer-made potpourri.

WHERE WILL YOU LOCATE?

Location may be dictated by a property that you or your family already own. But if you are starting out without such constraints, consider both traffic and image, among other requirements.

The Mall

Traffic at a mall may be excellent. The mall management will be able to tell you what the demographics of the market area are. Decide whether they fit your likely customer base. If your nearest mall attracts mostly retired people who are using it as their social outlet and your main customer base is aged thirty to fifty, the traffic might not be a particular help to you. Rent is almost certain to be high, though it may be negotiable. The greatest problem for you may be the hours. Mall leases state the hours and days when every store must be open. If you can't handle running a store that's open twelve hours a day, seven days a week, the mall isn't for you.

The Town

Is Main Street dead or dying, with poor parking accommodations and little traffic? Rents may be low, but traffic is low also. Will you be the only charming store on the street? Will you be enough of a magnet to draw out a sufficient number of customers? Perhaps the answers will be in your favor. Investigate further.

The Suburbs

Zoning against home-based businesses is usually very strict. Before you redecorate your garage into a charming shop, check out the regulations, as well as the feelings of your neighbors. Even if the zoning is legal, the neighbors might be against it, and vocally so. Instead, look for a commercial property in a shopping district within the suburb. Often old homes have been converted into commercial establishments, and you may find one perfect for you. If you are looking for a property to buy, there may be a converted apartment upstairs that would carry part of the mortgage payment.

The City

Is there traffic all day? Who is shopping and what are they buying? Does the location attract office workers who clear out right after work? Is the location dead on weekends? ᖗ **Ask the local merchants' association for more information on the trends in the district.** Remember, though that it is in the interest of the association to try to attract more business to the area. Also talk to some of the other shop owners who might attract a similar clientele.

The Country

An herb and flower business nestles into the country as if it belongs. It does. Here, being off the beaten track works in your favor. Many times I have more "outsiders" in my shop than locals. Now that my mailing list has grown dramatically, it is relatively inexpensive to market directly to people within a sixty-mile radius. At the start of each workshop in my barn, I ask people to introduce themselves, tell of their flower and herb interests, and where they are from. Frequently, 75 percent of the class is from more than twenty miles away.

Coming to the country to take a class or to buy flowers feels right, looks right, and on a warm summer's evening even smells and sounds right as the meadow scents drift into the barn and the crickets chirp their songs.

Rents are usually low, but good directions, maps, and signs take on added importance, as roads are unlit and street signs may be nonexistent.

WHEN WILL YOU BE OPEN?

Whether you plan to work at this business part-time or full-time, the shop needn't be open full-time. You can use several days each week to create more merchandise, make and ship custom orders, and attend workshops, classes, and trade shows. When you are deciding on your initial schedule, include at least one weekend day. Start with fewer hours and add on as you determine the need; reversing the procedure is deadly. Don't start out with too many hours and then cancel some. Your customers will be confused, disappointed, and angry, and you will give the impression that business is faltering. An example would be to start with Thursday, Friday, and Saturday from 11 A.M. to 5 P.M. Add evening hours on Friday and Saturday from after Thanksgiving till December 23. A couple from Virginia close their successful shop in the country for January, February, and March. They take their annual vacation after an excruciatingly busy Christmas season, then totally redecorate the shop, design new merchandise, do a little writing, and plan their year's special festivals and events. When April comes and their garden is again ready for planting, they open with renewed eagerness to sell their wares.

Choose regular hours and have someone available no matter what. Close only in the direst emergencies and at your peril. That means if you leave to sell at a crafts or flower show, the shop remains open.

ESTIMATING START-UP COSTS

Your business is meant to grow, not to spring up overnight in full bloom. It may take five years to reach your initial sales goal. In the meantime, your profits are determined by your expenses as well as by your sales. Economize where you can, but if you cut your advertising and promotions budget too much, few will find you and you will have no sales. If you have too little stock to choose from, patrons will not make return visits.

Examine the following list of start-up costs and calculate the amount of cash you will need to operate for a year. Fill in accurate numbers where you can and estimates where you can't. Where you must guess, research as much as you can, then choose a number on the high side. Discovering six months later that you allowed too much for expenses will give you a small working cushion; discovering that you allowed too little may put your cash flow in a disastrous state and put you out of business. Be prepared!

Onetime Expenses

Deposits and installation fees for phone and other utilities

Equipment, such as cash register, computer, and fax. (Don't rush out to buy these at first, but consider as possibilities.)

Licenses and permits

Remodeling, refurbishing, relighting the storefront, including permits for the work. (Paint is the cheapest way to add interest and excitement to interior decor.)

Security deposit

Storefront sign. (This must be professionally done. Check local regulations for size and style.)

Directional signs, necessary when you are off the beaten track

Store fixtures. (Use paint and fabric to give a cohesive theme to an odd assortment of hand-me-downs.)

Recurring Expenses (Monthly)
Bank and credit card fees
Business taxes
Loan repayment
Losses due to theft, breakage, and general old age of merchandise. Have regular sales or an ongoing sale corner. Refurbish once-beautiful flowers that have become tired looking.
Phone
Rent
Utilities, such as heat, water, electricity, and trash
Wages—yours and others

Recurring Expenses (Yearly)
Advertising, yellow pages
Advertising, year-round. (Check with local media on special rates for recurrent ads.)
Craft supplies and equipment: hot glue guns, clippers, pins and wire, wreath forms, and so on
Garden supplies and seeds
Insurance: fire and theft of fixtures, merchandise, and building, liability, vehicle, plate glass; umbrella policy if you are an individual proprietor
Merchandise
Postage and shipping; COD charges
Professional fees: accountant, lawyer, bookkeeper, graphic designer, computer helper
Public relations. (You should be able to do most of this yourself.)
Shop supplies, bags, tissue, boxes
Special events and promotions, advertising and direct expenses
Stationery and cards, printing, newsletters
Subscriptions and memberships (One of the cheapest and best means of continuing to learn your craft and business)
Travel to trade shows, workshops, and professional meetings. (Don't skimp here, as these are necessary for your own in-service training, professional development, and inspiration.)

Vehicle expenses. (Do you really need a different vehicle or will your old one do until you are ready to trade it in?)

WHERE YOU CAN SAVE

You can save money by using part of your own property. Not only will you have no outlay for rent and security and a reduction on utilities, but you also will have a likely deduction on your personal income taxes on home office, workshop, and retail space. Check on the latest IRS regulations for specifics.

If you are renting, select a site with minimum square footage, which will look chock full with less merchandise, rather than trying to transform a bowling alley into a bountiful market. Even in my huge barn, I opened it a section at a time as the need grew. Negotiate with the landlord. Don't accept the first rental figure. Check which insurances and utilities are included, which painting and remodeling fees he will absorb, and who will own the fixtures when the lease is up.

Make fixtures out of found materials and transform them with paint in your preferred colors. For example, check out your local electric company or electric supply store for rough wooden cable reels, which make superb display tables and are usually free for the asking.

Use a cash box from the hardware store instead of a fancy cash register.

Enlist help from family and friends. Allow them to put their talents to use, perhaps with computer expertise or carpentry and repainting.

Save your money in preparation for opening and eliminate bank interest. Borrow from yourself or from family at more favorable terms. Loans from banks are expensive to repay.

Select your business bank carefully; compare monthly banking fees and negotiate credit card fees.

Check with one or more reliable insurance brokers on how you can save on all of your insurance policies by grouping them.

Avoid COD charges by establishing credit in advance where possible.

Minimize shipping charges for merchandise by ordering from nearby suppliers when possible.

Be prepared to work long hours to make your business profitable. Consider working part-time at your other job as you pay off some of the extraordinary expenses required the first year.

In hiring others, look for ways to trade perks for higher salary. For example, if most of your employees are working mothers, flexibility with hours may be as important as increased wages. Offer a nice employee discount on purchases made for themselves or to give as gifts.

If you don't already own a computer, rent computer time at Kinko or other copy outlets for mailing-list maintenance, accounts, or other needs.

You probably can't get a listing in the yellow pages (vital) without a business phone line. If your store is at home, consider removing your residential phone to save the cost of one line. (Forget this suggestion if you have teenagers.)

Try classified ads instead of display ads, especially for sales and special events.

Hand-color printed fliers and newsletters to make them stand out from the crowd, especially those going to media representatives. (Now that my newsletter mailing list has gotten too big to totally hand-color, I have a VIP list of about fifty who get my special watercolor productions.)

Use bulk mailing rates where feasible; **Ask about using your printer's mailing permit.** He will probably charge you only for the actual postage, and you save the fees involved.

Instead of imprinting bags and gift boxes separately, compare prices for printed stickers that you can affix to cartons, boxes, bags, or anything else. Get an ink stamp with your logo as an even less expensive alternative.

Affix professionally designed vinyl letters to your personal vehicle to transform it instantly into a business wagon. You advertise wherever you drive.

CASH FLOW

Cash goes out as you pay expenses and comes in as people pay for their purchases or pay you a speaking or writing fee. This movement of money is called cash flow and is vital in every business. A positive cash flow means that you have enough money to cover all of your expenses, with more money flowing in than out. A negative cash flow means your bills will go unpaid for a while; you may pile up interest payments. If bills remain unpaid for too long, you will be out of business, even if you can show that you have accounts receivable to cover.

In the literature on starting a business, I found recommendations for start-up capital to cover anywhere from six months to three years. You have no doubt read many times that one of the primary reasons businesses fail is that they are underfunded from the start. That is, the owner incurs more expenses at the beginning when she has little income and doesn't have sufficient funds to continue to pay expenses until her income increases later. Put another way, there is a negative cash flow for too long, without the backup capital to cover.

Consider the retail florist business. The peak selling times occur at holidays, like Mother's Day, Valentine's Day, Christmas, Easter, and Thanksgiving. Florists tide themselves over with wedding and funeral work. The recently created Secretaries Week (initially Secretaries Day) was a major effort by floral marketers to increase the cash flow between major holidays. Note that as the dates of Easter vary, so too does Secretaries Week, to ensure that it falls at a fallow period. Expenses pile up before each holiday as the florist places orders anticipating sales. With thirty to sixty days' good credit from the flower wholesaler, the retailer expects that many sales will generate immediate cash or immediate bank credit from credit card customers. Thus she will have the positive cash flow enabling her to pay when her bills fall due.

As with retail florists, you will take every advantage of holiday sales and should create some of your own special events during the slow periods. If you have events the same time each year, customers will begin to look forward to your treats and plan for it in their calenders. Teas, May Day treats, First Harvest Festival, Pumpkin Patch Parties, historic commemorations—seek a theme to start a new tradition.

Think of the nature of the business you have or will have. Are you in an area with a definite tourist season? On Block Island or Cape Cod your shop may only be open three months out of the year. Some boutique owners have shops in northern areas for the summer season and southern areas for the winter tourist season. Do you expect that you will have heavy sales in the last quarter of the year, because of the Christmas season, or the traditional increase and interest in dried flower sales in the fall? The general trend is that gift-type shops sell 65 to 75 percent of their volume in the last quarter. If you live in the North and open your doors for the first time on January 2, you may wait until September for your sales to perk up. Your cash reserve must account for the flow, mostly *out* for nine months until it starts coming *in*.

Stock turnover is critical. Make it; sell it; earn money to buy more materials or merchandise; pay your bills; reap a profit. Until you sell it, you can't make or buy more. When merchandise fails to turn over, be ruthless; put it on sale; change it; take it apart and keep the good stuff; or toss it. Everyone makes mistakes in buying as well as mistakes in creating. What you felt was an innovative swag design may be appreciated but not purchased. An expensive wreath languishes on the wall. Our business is one of perishables. Unlike the baskets, containers, and other "hard goods," flower and herb materials will fade and lose their fragrance and taste.

If merchandise is not selling well, plan to move it around the store every two or three weeks, just as you move arrangements in a show booth to a better position. Add a label or a name for your composition to make it more immediately identifiable. I made a novel wreath for a book photograph from oregano and purple basil and trimmed it with dried hot peppers and tomatoes and a "bow" of tricolored fettucini. In my shop, the wreath attracted little attention as my customers failed to identify the dried herbs. After three weeks, when I got tired of seeing the wreath and began to worry about its shelf life, I concocted a sign and identifying label. It was no coincidence that the Pasta Wreath sold the next day.

Have a giant clearance sale going from one season to the next; reduce prices by 25 to 35 percent; then increase the discounts. Have a permanent sale nook for year-round bargains. Try not to hold over materials to the next year. Don't waste precious storage space with goods that are not up to your standards nor up to the latest trends.

CONSIGNMENT BUYING

In the next chapter, on wholesale markets, you'll learn why it is to your disadvantage to sell your own designs on consignment: in short, because the advantages are all with the shop owner. If you own the shop, however, the advantages are yours.

Say an artisan who specializes in wildflower and herb swags offers you her wares on consignment. You pay nothing for the goods until they are sold, then only pay the crafter at the end of the month. You can pick what you want from her many designs, choosing the strongest for your store. You work with the artisan to set the price (though she has the last word) and can reject any items that you feel are too expensive for your market or opt to try a few in the upper range as an experiment. You select enough items to make a display, placing them wherever they best fit in with the rest of your merchandise. You can get rid of them at no cost to you if they don't sell. You fill shop space with a quality product, yet don't own the product and aren't responsible for damage or theft. You get a commission for selling, now typically 40 to 50 percent. The main disadvantage in accepting crafts on consignment is that you must do the paperwork. Each artisan must receive a letter setting out the explicit terms of acceptance, such as that she must pick up wares within two weeks of notification; she can't withdraw items without a month's notice to you; and merchandise is left at her own risk. You must also list each item that you choose and its retail price as established by the crafter. You both sign the letter. You tag each item with a code number and mark it off on the master list when it sells. At the end of the month, you send a check to each artisan for the works that sold, less your commission.

SHOP DISPLAY

Lighting

When you've decided on your overall image and the marketing niche that you want to fill, you still must make the interior of the shop inviting, a place where customers delight in coming. With dried flowers and herbs, lighting is particularly important. Dried materials lack the glistening qualities of fresh petals and reflect much less light. What seems like enough ambient light for most purposes is far too little to highlight your dried flower crafts. Arrange for spotlighting, which has the flexibility of being moved as you redesign your displays. The spotlighting highlights certain section of the store and certain products like nothing else can. Your special products will radiate a healthy glow that makes them look more lively and less dead.

Vignettes

Rather than scatter all your merchandise around the shop, cluster items according to themes to make them more appealing and easier for the customer to admire. Each grouping is a vignette or tells a small story. The feature can be a holiday, a color theme, or even a particular flower. Pansies are beloved flowers in the garden. If you design a new line featuring pansies dried in silica gel, group the pansy wreaths and swags together along with some note cards with pansy faces, and baskets in an array of purples. If you have pansy-scented essential oils, include them as well.

Perhaps you have been designing with a new material like corrugated cardboard and have a huge roll from which you are working. Stand the roll up to use as a small table, hang above it your new square wreath forms and baskets formed of corrugated cardboard, along with merchandise featuring brown craft paper, twigs, and other naturals. Use large pieces of sheet moss to cover table or counter surfaces. Splash the whole vignette with several other earth colors or add moss-covered items. Find a small downed tree in the woods, drag it home, and wedge it into a clay pot to frame the vignette.

In each vignette, exhibit merchandise at different price levels; include a very expensive show-off piece, some items that you know will sell readily, and some less expensive impulse items with the same theme. The more expensive pieces help to sell the other goods by placing them in excellent company.

Fixtures

The best fixtures are versatile, readily movable, and relatively unobtrusive. You need provisions for hanging articles on the walls, suspending them from above as well as laying them on shelves of different heights. A small riser or pedestal, such as an overturned wooden box, can lift an item above the ordinary by changing display levels. Some manufacturers sell fixtures that work with their goods at reduced prices. F. O. Merz and Co. in Cowpens, South Carolina, has been running an ongoing special: Buy a preselected assortment of baskets and receive a vertical black metal tree from which to hang the whole assortment. Gilberties Herb Farm of Easton, Connecticut, sells handy natural wood display racks to house their small bottles of essential oils.

Color

The cheapest way to add pizazz to a display is by the use of color, using paint or draped fabric. Backdrops painted fuchsia, orange, and gold look right for the heat of summer, highlighting your sunflower vignette. The same backdrops in white, silver, and cobalt are ready for a winter's tale.

Props

Keep props to a minimum, only a suggestion of an idea. The more clever the prop and the more alluring the display fixture, the more the customer's eye is distracted from your wares. Sometimes I purchase display pieces and actually put price tags on them, like a reproduction carriage and sled that I bought one Christmas. If I sell a piece, I'm happy; if not, I'll use it again the next year and, if possible, for other occasions. The carriage, for example, is brought out for Mother's Day and again for a bridal display.

Junk can often be transformed into wonderful display props and backgrounds. In the farthest reaches of my barn stood old doors, shutters, and windows that were replaced by more functional pieces decades ago. The doors on trestles became tabletops, and the shutters stood on end became backgrounds to separate the sales floor from storage areas. The shutters don't match each other; there seem to be three different vintages. None have resale value or, with their gouges and broken slats, could be considered functional as shutters, but for my purposes they're perfect. Their aged paint sets off the colors in my spring wreaths. In the treasure trove I also found two small window frames with many of the panes intact. Set up in a V shape, they became backgrounds for garlands or swags. My clever assistant, Toni Groff, suspended small items by ribbons in the sections where the panes are missing, creating a mobile effect. What was a defect became a feature!

Customers often ask to buy antique display pieces, and I have been tempted to shop the antique markets specifically for the purpose of resale. This is a possible niche for someone, but not for me, as my path now leads in other directions.

BUYING MERCHANDISE

When you discover that it is impossible to stock your store solely with handmade products of one person—yourself—you can either hire more workers to help create more wares or buy other goods wholesale.

I used to think it was cheating if I designed with and sold any flowers and herbs that I didn't grow myself. But eucalyptus, gardenias, sarracenias, artichokes, pomegranates, pepperberries, and proteas can't grow in a Zone 6 garden in Orwigsburg, Pennsylvania. The list of impossibles continues with many other materials from arid climates and the warm tropics. And while my German statice is nicer than any I've seen, my colored statice is often spindly compared with the California product. Now I grow what I can and buy what I need, specializing in those varieties that I have learned through experience will grow easily in my garden. Other flowers that I can grow, but not in sufficient quantities, I buy fresh and dry myself. Peonies treated that way are far less expensive than any dried peonies I can buy shipped in from Holland.

As you begin to buy containers and other nonfloral items, it's easy to be confused by the range of products available. Visiting a major trade show like the International Gift Show in New York leaves you in a spin.

When possible, it is better to minimize the number of vendors you buy from than to scatter your orders around. Each order that comes into your shop must be unpacked, checked against the packing slip, shelved, and the bill paid. Each additional vendor increases the shipping and receiving costs. Think of the time and cost just paying another invoice. It may be best, for example, to resist the temptation of choosing your favorite ribbon patterns from many manufacturers' patterns and instead select all of your ribbon from one or two main vendors.

It is to your benefit to establish a personal relationship with the salesperson or sales rep of a vendor. She is a source of valuable information on best-selling products, changes expected in the line, special pricing, and the like. Compared with those of other customers, your orders may be inconsequential to a manufacturer; try not to dilute the spending power you have by scattering your orders among vendors. When you and the sales rep have an ongoing relationship, you will get help when you need rush orders or special requests.

On the other hand, if you do place all your orders with one vendor, what happens if the vendor becomes unreliable, can't fill an order, or goes out of business? You're left short until you can scurry around and replace it. This dilemma particularly affects those working with fresh flowers. If you have a party to decorate and at the last minute your regular wholesaler can't come up with the miniature pineapples that were to be the stars of your centerpieces, it's panic time. It's best to keep vendors to a minimum, to contain costs and improve your business relationship, but at the same time give yourself several options you can call on if needed.

CUSTOMER SERVICE
"May I help you?"

"I'm just looking."

That exchange is repeated in shops across America millions of times a day. All of your marketing efforts, your advertising, and your public relations campaigns are dedicated to bringing the customer into the shop. When the customer enters, you have a chance to complete the process with a sale. "I'm just looking" pushes the salesperson away, usually marking the end of the interaction. The customer is telling you to get lost.

Instead, greet the customer on entering the shop. No secretarial or restocking task is more important than taking care of the customer. If you had a slow morning and are just starting to unload your new baskets onto the shelves, invite the customer to come over to look at the fresh new items you are just putting out. She is the first one to see your new line, so ask her opinion. If you are designing a new wreath in your workshop area, ask her advice on whether a bow is a necessary adjunct. Let her see it with and without, and honor her opinion, at least for now. Your customers will be a source of excellent information and ideas. Some will know more about the flowers and herbs than you do. If you just picked a small wild pod and haven't yet identified it, involve your customer in the identification; if she knows the answer, you'll both be thrilled, and if she doesn't, she's no worse off than you, the "expert."

If you see a person looking at a particular item, go up to her and start to talk about it. When she fingers the *Nigella orientalis*, tell her it's a seedpod related to the love-in-a-mist that she might be familiar with. Show her the two together. Praise the sturdiness of the oriental nigella; demonstrate how she can change the look by opening one of the pods to enlarge the shape and extol the virtues of the pod sprayed a shimmery gold. After imparting your wisdom, step aside so that she doesn't feel pressured.

I think of selling as a teaching experience. I try to enhance the customer's knowledge about the product, whether she ultimately buys or not. I try to make it easy for the customers to ask questions by being willing to part with my "secrets." The reason her red roses always dry black is that she is starting with too deep a red variety; that sort will always dry black no matter how carefully processed. With relief she learns that it isn't her fault.

Seven Deadly Sins of Salesmanship

1. Failing to greet the customer when she enters the shop, ignoring her, chatting with employees, or gossiping on the phone.

2. Not knowing the product.

3. Failing to make suggestions for other items—floral foam for the arrangement, a pressed-flower gift card to go with the present, an extra bunch of foliage to enhance the flowers.

4. Overpromising: underestimating the time within which custom orders will be ready, exaggerating the ability of dried materials to withstand outdoor climates, or hyping the longevity of dried materials.

5. Failing to ask for the sale.

6. Failing to go beyond the sale: not getting her name and address for your mailing list, not mentioning your classes, not handing her a brochure about your next special event, lecture programs, and other services.

7. Failing to say "Good-bye, hope to see you again" to both buyers and nonbuyers.

Make the final transaction simple by accepting cash, check, and credit cards. I no longer ask for identification for personal checks, as I've had only one bad check in ten years. After you've been in business for a year or two and have a history of sales, make a determination about whether you need to require ID in your area. If you don't, it saves time and gives the customer the message that she is trustworthy. What a nice thought!

Wrap and pack efficiently in your special way and thank the customer for the transaction. If you exceed the customer's expectation in every respect, each one will pass the message along to others who will also become loyal fans.

HIRING HELP

At the beginning you may be working alone, or you may have recruited some family members to help with odd jobs. If your shop is open only several days a week, you may be able to handle all the work yourself, but as your business grows it will soon become clear that being the sole artisan, bookkeeper, advertising executive, secretary, buyer, and seller is too much. At this point, you will think of hiring help.

Your customers themselves are a great pool of potential help. The first screening is accomplished; you know they are interested because they visit your shop or enroll in your workshops. I have found that a want ad in the classifieds is not nearly as productive as a notice in the barn or an ad in my newsletter. Because my business is very small, and all of my workers are part-time, they must be able to change hats as the work demands. Creating arrangements is the glamour work; hand-weeding in the July heat and humidity or sweeping the barn floor is definitely not. In hiring, I want workers to know the bad news first and not to fantasize about the glamorous aspects of the business. Here's my favorite ad, which produced my two best all-time workers:

> **HELP!**
> **Wanted.** Hot, dirty, sweaty glorious work. Weed, plant, harvest, sell, create. Need a strong back and a positive outlook. Will teach everything else. Permanent part-time. Approx. 15 hours weekly.

Inspiring Your Workers

Being in the flower and herb business has a great advantage. You are not selling shoes or auto parts, but a product beloved by many. In your immediate locale I can promise you there are myriad people who wish they were doing what you are doing. They just want to be around the herbs and flowers. You may not be able to offer much more than minimum wage at first, but it turns out that for many, money is quite far down on the list of satisfactions. You may be able to offer the flex time appreciated by most young parents. You must offer some education and training. You can offer some other perks, like employee discounts on purchases for their own use and free bouquets of fresh flowers from the cutting beds when you're over-stocked. When interesting opportunities occur, include an employee as a way of recognizing ability. I sometimes invite an employee on a buying trip to a gift show (especially nearby ones where expenses will be minimal). I lay out my goals for the trip and my budget, and encourage her to scan the merchandise with me in the treasure hunt for that elusive object, the perfect item. Imagine her delight if I purchase the item for the store and it sells well. She is now part of the process and has a vested interest in the shop. If the item doesn't sell well, make sure she knows it was ultimately your decision, so she is not to blame. It will go on sale with a few of your other miscalculations.

There is no better positive reinforcement than taking ideas seriously. Listen to suggestions and ideas of your employees and incorporate the best into your business. Reward their hard work.

A student has spent many summers loyally toiling in my garden, growing up amid my perennial borders. As we shot the photographs for my second book of floral designs in the barn, I invited him to watch for a while and introduced him to the crew. When writing the acknowledgments to those who had contributed to the growth of the business and the book, I included his name. Feedback from neighbors indicated that he was flashing the book proudly around Orwigsburg, and he confessed to me that he had displayed it to his girlfriend's parents, official recognition in

WHERE TO FIND TRAINING COURSES FOR YOU AND YOUR STAFF

• Horticultural trade associations such as the International Herb Growers and Marketers Association and regional growers' associations, on all aspects of the herb and flower business

• Regional florist associations, on design, trends, and marketing

• Lectures and demonstrations at flower shows, on arranging, design, trends, and gardening; usually included with the price of admission

• Annual meetings of Garden Clubs of America and Herb Society of America, on gardening and design

• Lectures and symposia at gift shows on marketing, packaging, display, trends, and sales

• State horticultural societies, botanical gardens and arboretums, garden and flower design beginner to master classes, state cooperative extension services, on growing, small business, marketing, and design ❧

black and white. The flower and herb business may not make huge profits but there is great satisfaction in intangibles.

Training

In my want ads I generally don't require experience with flowers. I am, however, interested in an artistic eye, that elusive quality that allows people to notice the best quality and select the finest designs. At the Meadow Lark Flower & Herb Farm we sell almost no dyed or painted materials except at Christmastime. I have tried floral paints on many products and am usually dissatisfied with the results. One trainee working on her first minibouquet selected from the bins of small flowers every painted experiment I hadn't yet discarded. Her mechanical technique was fine, but she needed to be redirected toward choosing better-quality flowers.

Part of the training is in sales techniques and part in familiarity with common and botanical names, as customers will request items by either. Signs and labels are a tremendous help to both customers and inexperienced sales help. Most of the questions get repeated over and over again, and your help will learn from hearing the way you answer. Jewel Robinson, my chief of staff at the Philadelphia Flower Show, can give the most detailed directions to the farm, even though she's never been there. Her answers indicate an intimate knowledge of every important landmark as she invites customers to visit us in our natural setting.

Pass along the books, magazines, and journals that you buy, and discuss them with the staff afterward. Take employees with you or send them to professional seminars when these are offered at low cost. The more competent your employees feel to answer questions, the better they will feel about themselves.

Offer praise freely for jobs well done and to people who add an extra touch to the atmosphere in your shop.

CHAPTER FIVE

Selling Wholesale

A successful crafter, now a successful manufacturer, placed one appliqué pillow on consignment at a Woman's Exchange. Encouraged by her first swift sale, she went directly to a furniture store whose owner she knew and received an order for six pillows, her first wholesale sale. She now has a thriving wholesale business with customers around the country. Reflecting on why she chose to approach a store rather than go the route of retail crafts fairs, she said that she greatly preferred dealing with decisive professional buyers who have no time to lose, rather than retail customers who have trouble making up their minds. She felt it would be too annoying to sell retail; she never even considered it.

The concept of selling wholesale is simple. You produce quantities of wares and sell to stores, catalogs, and other outlets. You list your product, along with specifications like size, color, and price. You may set minimum dollar values or quantities for stores to order from you. The store buys your product and sets the retail price. Although in the gift industry "keystoning," or doubling the wholesale price, is an established practice, some stores in upscale areas and some posh catalogs may add a 150 or 200 percent markup, and some discount stores may sell your product for less. Your product may be selling at different prices at different outlets around the country.

Selling wholesale means casting a wide net for customers. You, however, are busy designing and producing your product and can't possibly devote as much time as is necessary to traveling and selling your wares. In addition, it would be far too expensive to traipse around the country with samples in tow hoping for enough sales to make the trip worthwhile. How do you as a small business owner find wholesale customers around the country? The two most common methods are finding sales representatives in areas where you want to sell and taking a booth at a wholesale gift show.

USING REPS

People who excel at selling can choose to make a career as a manufacturer's representative—a rep. Reps in the gift industry handle a number of gift lines from different manufacturers or craftspeople. They call on shop owners and try to sell your merchandise, as well as the other merchandise they represent, sending in any orders they receive. You handle the delivery.

For their services, reps now typically receive 15 percent of the money you get for the wares (gross excluding shipping). You must be in constant touch with your reps to make sure they understand and appreciate the quality and uniqueness of your line and are enthusiastic about selling it. Because their sole income is based on a percentage of sales, they want to represent only a "winning" line. If a rep thinks your prices are too high or too low, your product lacks quality or uniqueness, or directly competes with another product she represents, she will refuse to take on the line. Even worse, the rep may be enthusiastic at first with a new product but fail to keep pushing the line.

Reps cover a stated territory, like Northern California. You may need another rep in Southern California to cover the total state. Because your six styles of wreaths and four colors of swags are difficult to show from the back of a van stuffed with other products, some reps have their own permanent showrooms in the major market areas, like Atlanta, Chicago, and New York, and gift buyers make the trip several times a year to the showrooms to see the lines.

To find reps, look in the back of professional trade magazines like *Giftware News* or *Gifts & Decorative Accessories* under the classifieds for "gift lines wanted." Go to trade shows and look on the bulletin board for "lines wanted." Place your own notice in these locations. ᶜᵛᵛ **Ask shop owners you're friendly with about the best reps who call on their stores, and contact those reps directly.**

A specific agreement on the territory, the commission, ownership of the samples, and time of payment can avoid unpleasantness. It is common not to have a time limit on the agreement, so either party can get out of it easily if the product isn't selling. That should ensure no messy "divorce" between you and a rep.

DOING THE WHOLESALE SHOWS

Large shows around the country sell to the gift market and attract thousands of store buyers. The biggest are in New York, Los Angeles, Chicago, and Atlanta. There are many other important but smaller shows in Boston, Washington, Seattle, San Francisco, Denver, and King of Prussia, Pennsylvania. To shop the show you must have credentials indicating that you are a wholesale buyer, exhibitor, or member of the press. Always try to see a show before you invest your money in renting space. If you are a potential seller at the show, call the management in advance and ᶜᵛᵛ **ask for free admission on the basis of doing the show in the future.** Remember that management has to sell their floor space—a goal that coincides with your need to sell. Or ᶜᵛᵛ **ask an owner of a store where you shop if you can go to a show as her assistant to gain some experience.** (If she agrees, determine in advance what she wants from you, and don't annoy her or slow her down. She's there to accomplish her mission, and it's very hard work to shop a show.) Familiarize yourself with the floor layout and see where the dead space is, where buyers never seem to reach. In smaller shows, buyers walk the entire floor. In larger shows like the New York International Gift Fair—whose twenty-three hundred exhibits take up three floors of the mammoth Javits Convention Center and two passenger ship piers on the Hudson River—feet and shoulders grow weary before buyers have traversed all seven miles of aisles. Naturally, companies with longevity at the show get their first choice of spaces and if they like their spots can return there year after year, making it easier for customers to find them. But there are always dropouts: Companies come and go; people get sick at the last minute; other business crises occur; and you may have an opportunity to improve your location.

As you walk the show floor, make notes and evaluate the following to help decide whether to try to sell at that show:

1. Check out the competition. How many people are selling products in your category? Note the pricing of the products. Are your most important pieces priced in line with the competition and are your smaller pieces priced to sell quickly? Is your quality noticeably better, thereby justifing a higher price?

2. Do you have something new, a product that will distinguish your booth from others at the show?

3. Approach several booth holders at the show. Ascertain that they are the principal or sales managers, not temporary help. Find out how the show is going for them, how long they've been doing this show, and anything special you should know in trying to decide whether to participate. Ask your questions at off-peak hours, such as very early or very late in the day, and step aside as soon as a potential buyer enters the booth.

Also observe and make notes to help you if you decide to sell at any wholesale show.

Notice the design of the booths. Most are open to encourage customers to come in, walk around, and handle the products. See what seems to be the most effective way to display a product such as yours.

Observe how booths handle lighting. In most shows, the price of the booth rental includes only bare concrete floor space, some ugly draperies to define the booth space, and dim general lighting overhead. Note how some booths use good lighting to enhance the products.

Be aware of how some booth designers completely hide the mandatory draperies and create an ambience in the booth to high-light their products. In the best designs, the ambience creates a mood but is not more important than the merchandise itself, or customers will start wanting to buy the display cases.

Learn also from watching different styles of salesmanship. Observe how off-putting it is when the lone salesperson pays more attention to paperwork, her lunch, or her book than to you.

Talking with Show Management

∾ **Ask for attendance and sales figures for each show.** The Atlanta Gift Show, a hot spot for selling, has four main shows a year. The January and July shows are widely considered by booth holders to be the best; they refer to the off-peak shows as the "dog shows" because business is slower. Show management encourages vendors to exhibit in more than two shows by offering a point system. If you sell at more shows, you get extra points toward the choice of better booth locations. If you start with the spring show, expect slower sales than if your first show is in January. Ask for all of the necessary information.

∾ **Ask what the cancellation policy is.** Read the fine print of the contract.

Ascertain whether the show you want to do is a new show. If so ∾ **ask for a concession on price.** Promoters of new shows are eager to sell their space. It may take at least three years for a new show to establish its reputation and for word of mouth to reach store buyers. A new show may be easy to get into, but sales will be slower than at an established show.

It may seem impossible to gain admission to an established show. If you have a professional-looking press kit, now is the time to show it off. Send promotional materials about yourself and your products. Include publicity and newspaper features and photos of your work and display. Be persistent.

Convince show management that you can deliver on your orders and prepare to do just that. As a craftsperson starting out, you may be amazed by the success of your first show and receive orders beyond your hopes. You must be prepared with sources for materials and time to make your products. If you can't deliver as promised, customers will complain to show management and you will not be asked to return. Remember that word of mouth is effective in the negative as well as positive.

Can you make the extra effort necessary for last-minute (one to six weeks) attendance at a desirable show? If so, let management know that you are prepared to take a last-minute space if one becomes available. Once you're in, management won't forget you.

Talking with Shop Owners

Select several shops that seem to be good outlets for your products. Don't try to sell them anything—just concentrate on your research. ⌒ **Ask the owners or buyers which trade shows they attend and during what month they do most of their buying.** Inquire about which shows they've tried and don't go to anymore. Find out why not.

If you sell at a trade show, remember that store buyers are attracted to something new. Two gift shops on the charming but short main street of Clinton, New Jersey, do not want to be selling the same lines of merchandise. Some stores want an exclusive right to sell your product; some want a different design. Even if a store becomes your loyal customer and the buyer returns year after year, the first question is often "What's new?" When paper twist ribbon came on the market a few years ago, it was a hot item and appeared in many flower designs. Then the French imported wired ribbon with a silky look became hot, and everyone wanted to buy products incorporating that ribbon. In its turn, chiffon ribbon in shimmering colors became the new adornment for quality wreaths and arrangements. Just as grapevine gave way to wild huckleberry, then birch and manzanita, there are always new and exciting materials to incorporate into designs. As you design products for the show, be aware of them.

Wholesale buyers might be attracted to square- or diamond-shaped wreaths rather than round, or to arched rather than straight swags. Changing the look within certain parameters is the mission of most buyers, so keep abreast of the trends and showcase new styles at your booth.

For a detailed discussion on doing trade shows, see *How to Sell What You Make*, by Paul Gerhards.

SELLING WHOLESALE TO CATALOGS

Catalog buyers zip through trade shows scouting for next season's or next year's catalogs. They have a theme in mind, the look of a page, and prices for the items they want. They often expect special treatment, and because the potential is there for a big order, they often wrench concessions from the crafter. They will surely ask for a bigger discount and possibly some changes in design or packaging. They may ask you for an exclusive on the design or for an advertising fee. You, of course, must decide whether the changes or price reductions are worth it to you and still let you make a profit. If the catalog places an initial order with you, a backup order often goes along with it, as well as potential future delivery of even more goods. You must be capable of delivering the backup order almost immediately if sales are heavy. But if sales are weak, the catalog isn't obliged to take delivery of the backup. Will you be stuck with the extra raw materials? ∾ **Ask your supplier to reserve stock in case you need an immediate delivery,** so that you don't have to pay for the goods if you don't get the backup order.

Does the catalog have the look that you want for your craft? Do you want to be seen in their company? Having your craft in a catalog, if it's a good one, is often perceived as prestigious and can be used as a selling point with retail stores. Store owners usually don't see a catalog as direct competition because their customers can see and handle their products before buying and don't have to pay delivery or shipping charges. Catalog shopping can sometimes avoid state sales taxes that may add to the cost in a store, however.

CD-ROM

A full-page ad on the inside cover of *Crafts Report* solicits exhibitors for a wholesale "crafts trade show" on CD-ROM. The juried craftspeople who pay for this service will exhibit six images in an electronic "booth" as well as their order form. Orders will go directly to the crafter.

Craftproducers of Charlotte, Vermont, announces that CD-ROM will distribute free ten thousand disks to wholesale buyers. The opportunity to go on-line via the Internet is offered as a bonus.

Predictions from the computer world that people will be shopping on home computers are slow to be realized. As I write this manuscript, about 95 percent of the Internet users are male and about 95 percent of the retail buyers of flower crafts are female, a mismatch on the retail level, though that may change. On the wholesale level, there are many more businesspeople of both sexes conversant with computers. A CD-ROM crafts show is a promising concept that definitely bears watching and evaluating.

A COMPARISON

My first year in business I had both wholesale and retail customers in my own small experiment to see which would work better for me. My store buyers, pleased with sales, wanted to reorder more of exactly the same things. But I wanted to design and make unique arrangements. That would have involved sending photos or showing the store buyers the new wares, a time-consuming, expensive procedure. I soon dropped the wholesale customers and concentrated on retail, where I could continue to work out new designs and produce small numbers of each before changing to something else.

With wholesale you make more of each style and fewer one-of-a-kind items. That is an advantage or a disadvantage, depending on your preferences. Most people start designing and making something because of their desire to create and the pleasure in fabricating the piece. The farther you go in the wholesale market, the more you must produce, and the markup is smaller than in retail. The point comes at which you can no longer make all the pieces yourself. You may hire an apprentice to do the preparation, and still call yourself a craftsman if your hands are on each piece you turn out. But by the time you have five people working for you, you may simply be designing and making the prototypes; others are now fabricating all the pieces you sell. You are a designer-manufacturer, responsible for the business side of your operation and production, but no longer crafting the pieces.

At this juncture many craftspeople rebel, saying that this is not the reason they started the business. They experience a sense of loss when manual contact with making their wares is so limited. Others feel the thrill of creativity as the business grows and, while continuing to have an influence over the design, now get enjoyment from seeing a business that started with one small arrangement thrive and actually make money. If you don't want to leave the studio for the executive suite, selling retail may be for you. The markup is higher and the output can be lower.

Flower and herb growers who want to have a wholesale business selling their products must grow in quantity in order to have the volume needed for a wholesale markup. I was told by an extension agent that ten acres was a minimum planting area, justifying farm equipment, to have a wholesale flower business. Growers who plant an acre or two do not have the benefits of economy of scale and will probably have to sell retail or may have to buy many of their materials on the wholesale market.

If your business is pressed flowers and herbs, you can grow what you need in an ordinary garden rather than a farm. And if your business is small and part-time, of course, your needs will be smaller too.

In selling retail, you are constantly in touch with the buyers who will actually be placing your flowers in their homes. You receive direct and immediate feedback on what will work for them and what won't and can use that information in adapting your designs. I learned, for example, that a front door wreath must be thin enough to fit between the house door and storm door, and the dried materials must be sturdy enough to handle banging and slamming as the kids run in and out. When I sell a wreath I can give some instructions on care and handling or attach a care tag with the information. We have several designs that are specified as door wreaths, and other more fragile ones that we sell only if we hear the magic words "I want this for my wall."

When your creative level seems strangely depleted, retail customers can make suggestions or ask for custom orders that lead you to incorporate the product into the line. My workshop is in a public space where customers can see me create special orders. I narrate as I work, and often I get an order for a similar piece. Nothing makes an article more attractive than knowing that someone else wants it.

If you sell wholesale, on the other hand, your store buyers and reps give feedback and suggestions on design, because they feel they have an intimate knowledge of what the customer wants. Sometimes they do, and sometimes they are working from their own needs and interests, being one layer removed from the ultimate buyer. But the wholesale craftsperson's studio is private and secure from unexpected intrusions, and the style of working can be more remote—a blessing to many.

CHAPTER SIX

Selling Intangibles

Perhaps you think you are selling only flower and herb arrangements. Indeed you may start by selling your product but end by selling intangibles as well—your design skills, your knowledge, and your personality. Customers love to buy directly from the craftsperson because it brings them closer to the product. If they actually see you design and form the wreath at a demonstration and hear you talk about it, and perhaps about yourself, it seems almost as if they participated in the construction.

Sometimes in a demonstration I ask the audience for their opinions. Draping some ribbon around a wreath, I ask if they like it better with or without; holding up some miniature pumpkins sprayed gold, I ask whether these should be added to an arrangement as a finishing touch. The audience responses are *always* mixed. Sometimes I follow the will of the majority and sometimes my own preference, which may be in the minority. Either way I can make the point that tastes differ, and there is more than one way to make a lovely arrangement. Sometimes your opinion depends more on your momentary feelings and whether they are expansive or contemplative, celebratory or quiet, than on any elements of design.

Expertise comes by doing. You start by learning your craft, and with experience, observation, study, practice, and reworking comes skill. You may not put the label on yourself but others will. You are an expert in your field. You know about growing and drying, or you know about designing and arranging, or you know about selling; you know about cooking with herbs or their medicinal uses; you are a gardener who knows about landscape designs featuring herbs and flowers for drying; you create dramatic displays. You have all sorts of esoteric information that you may not even realize you have. You learn in formal education settings, but also by absorbing expertise through watching, reading, researching, and rehearsing. Get comfortable with the *expert* label because it means increased business for you. This is no time for false modesty or unnecessary humility. Learn to smile, say thank you, and appreciate the praise, even if the little voice inside is insisting that you are completely untrained.

SIX WAYS TO SELL YOUR EXPERTISE

1. Give Workshops at Your Studio
Taking into account the interests of your potential audience as revealed in questions you have received and products most admired, define the topics with which you feel most comfortable and most knowledgeable. Make a list of three to five topics to start, with brief descriptions.

In spring and summer 1995, Spoutwood Farm in Glen Rock, Pennsylvania, offered thirty-one classes, including An Aromatic Springtime Wreath, An Apple Branch Wall Hanging, Wild Medicinal Herb and Weed Encounter, Basketmaking—All Natural, and Candied Herbs and Violets Maytime Tea Party. The description of each class was so inviting that one wanted to dash off immediately to participate. Classes were led by the owners, Rob and Lucy Wood, as well as by visiting experts. The learning center brochure also included an invitation to the fourth annual Fairie Festival and other special events, a lot of power packed in a four-page brochure, mailed bulk rate to an extensive mailing list.

Check out the possibilities for free listings in your area, such as community calendars, and find out how much lead time they need. Workshops and other classes, because they are educational, may be eligible for free listings in newspapers and radio and TV calendars. Be sure to include your contact number, such as a phone or fax number, and an address for additional information. Pursue these resources avidly; miss no opportunity for free promotion in the prestigious media.

Advertise your series of classes or workshops together to save on costs, but price each individually. Consider offering a discount or incentive if people sign up for three or more of the series, or if more than three people sign up together. An incentive might be a 10 to 15 percent discount on any item, or on specific items purchased at the time of the class.

Set prices, including materials, that are realistic but profitable. When figuring your costs, don't forget setup and cleanup time and teaching time, as well as all materials.

Decide on the number of students you can accommodate, both in terms of space and in terms of the number you can oversee at once; ten to twelve is a good size for your first workshops and fifteen to twenty when you are more experienced. If you have an assistant who can help you and if you have plenty of elbow room, you can handle up to five additional students.

Take registrations in advance, with the full fee or 50 percent of the fee to secure a place. Have a stated refund policy for emergency cancellations, such as refund for credit only, refund less 20 percent, or other stated policy. If you take reservations with no advance payment, you will be very disappointed at the number of no-shows or people who call with last-minute changes of plans. "It was a beautiful day and I decided to play golf instead." With advance payment, there are few cancellations.

Some workshops will be much more popular than others, and it's often difficult to predict in advance which are which. Take names for a waiting list of the most popular workshops and offer a second date or repeat the workshop next season.

Although you have a maximum number, consider having no minimum number. Those who have signed up for a class, perhaps only five, will be very disappointed if you cancel, engendering some bad feelings. You want a reputation as a person who does what she says and knows how to handle her business.

Two years in a row I signed up to take a five-day nonfiction writing seminar sponsored by the Smithsonian Institution. The workshop was canceled each year, once after I had made nonrefundable plane reservations to the workshop site, and each time after I had blocked out time on my hectic schedule for the seminar. Needless to say, I would never sign up for a workshop with the Smithsonian again and asked that my name be withdrawn from the mailing list.

Time classes so that people in the work force can attend. They will probably make up a large portion of your audience. Either schedule only on evenings and weekends, or have a day class and repeat it in the evening.

2. Hold Workshops Away from Home Base

If you don't have your own area for workshops, consider renting space for the purpose in a nonprofit center like the local YMCA, the community center, an art center, or an adult education center. Costs will probably be lower than in a commercial establishment. In renting, you maintain control of all other aspects of the program, registration, and all the responsibilities for advertising and promotion, although the center may help publicize your program among their membership.

3. Offer Your Services to Adult Education Centers

An adult education center will advertise the classes, usually extensively, take care of registration, give you the space, and pay you a set fee. You bring the materials and supplies. The fee might be much less than you could make at home, but it's a place to start without outlay for rent and advertising. It also lends legitimacy to your enterprise.

4. Present Demonstrations

Most groups that ask you to speak will prefer a demonstration to a workshop, as the fee will usually be much less. At a demonstration, the speaker does all the work. Some of those attending will learn and attempt similar designs at home; others are simply looking for a social occasion and a pleasant afternoon's diversion.

At an hour-long demonstration, I typically make three or four designs and talk about the materials and the history or background of each. I answer questions as I go rather than at the end, as I am seeking an informal give-and-take where both the audience and I can relax and have fun.

Set your demonstration fee in advance and state it to the host group. Keep travel expenses separate. Key the cost of mileage to IRS reimbursement schedules. If you must stay overnight, the host group should be responsible for the expenses.

Don't be overly concerned that some sponsoring groups are working for a charity. Most groups looking for programs are trying to earn money for worthy causes. If you feel you must reduce your fee for every worthy cause, stay out of the demonstration business because you will actually lose money.

Determine in advance who owns the finished pieces. Fresh flower arrangers often include a charge for the wholesale cost of the flowers. Then the sponsor owns the arrangements to raffle off or dispose of them as preferred. Since dried materials aren't perishable, I choose not to charge extra for the materials, and I keep ownership of the arrangements. I can then try to sell them after the demonstration or take them home to sell at some other time.

Take some extra items along to a demonstration to sell. Perhaps bunches of dried materials, including any distinctive ones you will be using that day, extra containers if unusual, or special forms or mechanical devices you plan to demonstrate with. In my first demonstration, I brought antique containers from my collection, and everyone clamored to buy them. In my second demonstration, I used a lovely red lacquer basket from my shop, but I had only one. Now I select unusual containers from my stock and always sell a few at each event.

Also offer for sale any books or pamphlets you have written. Authors who self-publish find speaking engagements an excellent venue for distributing their books.

Have handouts about your subject. Always include your name, address, phone number, and the copyright symbol, which will help protect your hard work.

Plan to accomplish at least three goals at the demonstration in addition to the stated purpose of getting paid to give a presentation. Make additional sales and gather names for your mailing list. Take your workshop schedule for the season and get recruits. Hand out your newsletter, card, or literature about your future events. Members of your audience belong to other groups and will pass your name around for future work.

5. Become a Consultant

Once you become an expert in what you do, you will get calls, letters, and drop-ins asking for your help and advice. When I started my business I was exceedingly generous with my time, spending hours with people who would tour my farm and ask me what, when, where, why, and how. I certainly didn't have all the answers, maybe not even half of the answers, but I knew lots more than my questioners. Having been both a teacher and a psychologist, my whole bent, training, and experience was in helping others to learn.

It slowly dawned on me how much time I was taking out of my workday giving advice. I changed my tactics. Now I answer one or two questions if I don't consider them of proprietary interest; for example, I always tell people where to find seeds for particular cultivars and always answer to the best of my ability at lectures and workshops. But if someone pops up requesting my time or appears at a busy show asking questions when I'm trying to wait on customers, I give them my card and offer my consultation service by appointment. Whether in person or long-distance by telephone, I briefly describe my services and my fees. Those who understand that professionals don't give away free services, who expect to pay the accountant for setting up their books, the lawyer for advice on business structure, the PR person for promoting their product, or the rep for selling it, will understand why you need to charge for consultation and will make their own determination as to whether it is worth it to them. If not, you have your time back to use as you wish.

Craftspeople have traditionally been very helpful to each other, giving tips on how to handle certain shows, sharing experiences with collections, and watching each other's booths during break times. Potters don't, however, share the formula for new glazes they took great pains to formulate. Continue to be helpful in ways that don't give away too much of your time or your trade secrets. You are the sole judge of this.

Remember that some people make a living as business consultants, helping small businesses get started or evaluating businesses for future growth. Consultation, once you have the expertise, is a way for you to gain additional income from your knowledge and experience.

Give workshops on business practices, teach classes, have private sessions, and write articles about your experiences. You worked long and hard to get where you are. If you are in business, then think like a professional. This book is my way of using my business experience to help, at low cost, those wanting to start a business or make one flourish.

6. Become a Writer, Illustrator, or Photographer

As you amass more and more information about your specialty, consider writing as a way to earn money from your craft. Gain confidence by writing short pieces gratis.

Write a newsletter for your customers as a publicity and promotion piece. Along with news of your workshops, shows, and special events, include at least one informational piece on a topic of interest. One of mine from a recent newsletter appears on page 95.

From the Farm

MEADOW LARK FLOWER & HERB FARM ORWIGSBURG, PA

HARVEST OPEN HOUSE

The Great Barn
at
Meadow Lark Farm

10 am to 4 pm
Rain or Shine

Refreshments
Demonstrations:11am
Continuous Videos
of Floral Design

Sat, Aug 31, Sun & Mon, Sept. 1,2
Sat & Sun Sept. 7 & 8
Sat & Sun Sept 14 &15
Sat & Sun Sept. 28 & 29

87 varieties dried flowers
fragrant and culinary herbs
mixed bouquets & wreaths
potpourris
unusual baskets
arrangements
pressed flower frames
special orders
topiary & garlands
floral books & videos

From the Farm
Volume 1, Number 2
Fall 1991

From the Farm is published periodically
by Meadow Lark Flower & Herb Farm
for distribution to its customers.

FALL WORKSHOPS

Pressed Flowers
Learn how to press flowers to retain their shape and color.
Practice some elements of design with pressed flowers.
Make a floral picture, note cards, or floral frame.
Wed. Sept. 25, 1-3:30 **or**
Wed. Sept. 25, 7-9:30 $30

Fall Harvest Wreath
Choose from a bountiful array of dried sunflowers, gloriosa
daisies, bittersweet, Japanese lanterns, okra pods,
mini-pumpkins, wheat, martynia pods, multi-colored yarrows,
tansy, safflower, sorghum and other materials.
Learn to design and fashion a wreath on a natural
vine frame. Completed wreath will be 16-18"
Wed. Oct 2,1-3:30 **or**
Wed. Oct 2, 7-9:30 $30

Herbal Tea Wreath
Combine tea herbs like chamomile, applemint, and
bergamot with dried rose hips, dried wild raspberries
and other delicious materials to make a lovely
14" wreath. Complete the project with a tea strainer
or infuser. Perfect to hang in your kitchen or
give as a gift.
Sat Oct 5, 9:30-12 **or**
Sat Oct 5, 1-3:30 $35

Dried Topiary Designs
Make a topiary of dried flowers, herbs, and berries
in an old terracotta pot. Will stand about 14" high when
complete, perfect for end table or decorative accent.
Wed. Oct 9, 1-3:30 **or**
Wed. Oct 9, 7-9:30 $40

Holiday Decorations with
Natural Materials
Ellen Platt will present decorations for home,
door and table with natural fresh and dried materials.
Easy to make projects combining available fruits
and flowers. See demonstrations of projects from her
forthcoming book for Rodale Press,
FLOWER CRAFTS FROM A COUNTRY GARDEN.
Demonstration $15

You can show editors brief articles like this as samples of your writing even if you have never been published anywhere. Also use this type of writing to hone your skills of being informative yet concise.

Write a pamphlet to illuminate material you discuss in your lectures. Perhaps a compendium of your favorite herbal recipes, perhaps a series of tips on incorporating herbs into the landscape or into fresh flower arrangements. Whatever it is, if it's original, design it nicely on your computer and print it. Offer it for sale at a reasonable price in your shop, booth, or at workshops and demonstrations that you give. This is called self-publishing. Put your logo, name, address, and phone and fax numbers on the pamphlet, as they should be included on all printed materials you produce. Be sure to put a copyright symbol © on all your written work. This symbol alone can protect you from the theft of your words without your writings being officially registered in Washington.

Write short articles for your local newspaper. ᥫᥬ **Ask neighborhood newspapers about their publishing policy and whether they accept freelance articles.** Perhaps the local advertising tabloid circulated free will accept an article but won't

HYDRANGEAS
DRYING TIPS
from
The Meadow Lark
Flower & Herb Farm

The trick to drying hydrangeas successfully is in knowing when to pick them. If you pick hydrangeas early they will shrivel, rather than retain their shape when dried. If you pick them too late, they will lose their glorious color and turn brown. Pick blue or white hydrangeas when they are fully mature, after the color starts to change. Blue hydrangeas change to a lavender blush in August, white hydrangeas flush with pink and burgundy in September. The petals should feel papery to the touch and rustle slightly. The exact timing depends on weather conditions so continue to check every few days. If picked at the proper time, no hanging is necessary. Just arrange in a basket or use in a wreath and the flowers will complete their drying in situ.

pay. Use the opportunity to write something informational—for example, something about preserving wedding bouquets—not a puff piece for your shop. Your business name and shop or contact address may bring you new customers.

Scan some of your favorite magazines that publish articles in your specialty on flowers and herbs. Check out the letters to the editor section or the readers' suggestion column. When you see an opportunity to respond to an article or submit a tip, send it in. *Victoria* magazine started a "Reader to Reader" section for buying and publishing observations from readers. Note the length and tone of the published items and make a submission. When writing to a magazine, be sure to include your business name and address.

Freelance writing. If you are ready to become a professional freelance writer on your subject, borrow this year's *Writer's Market* from your library. Familiarize yourself with this excellent resource. It lists almost all the periodicals in this country, whether they accept freelance work, what type of article they publish, the address, how to submit, whether they demand a query letter first, and the range of fees. Periodicals listed range from general interest to highly specialized ones you have never heard of. Study the section on query letters. You need to write a brief, snappy summary of the proposed article and title, piquing the interest of the editor and whetting her appetite for more. Along with the query letter, submit a short résumé of your credentials, including a list of any other writings and reproductions, if possible. Each author must take a first step when she has nothing else to show. As you build up a bibliography, acceptance becomes easier and easier. In publishing there are famous stories of manuscripts getting rejected over and over until one publisher sees the light or the author self-publishes. One such story involves the author Richard Paul Evans and his book *The Christmas Box*, which he wrote for his two young daughters in 1994. He had twenty copies privately printed to distribute to his family, and when people started making requests to bookstores, he had more printed and distributed but could find no regional publisher among all that he tried. His book went on to make the New York

Times paperback best seller list and sold four-hundred thousand copies by Christmas of that year, when it was finally sought after by commercial publishers and movie studios.

An agent can spare you many rejection letters by resubmitting the manuscript or proposal until you get a favorable response. Remind yourself that persistent people make their own luck.

Before you travel along the book-publishing highway, read *How to Get Happily Published*, by Judith Appelbaum. She takes you through the steps from the book proposal to postpublication publicity—it's a bible for first-time authors.

Some books are published as work-for-hire (sometimes called fee-for-service). Books in the Ortho gardening series, available in many garden centers, are like that. The publisher selects an author and contracts with the author for a one-time fee, regardless of the number of copies the book sells. There are no royalties.

Sometimes the name of the author is listed in work-for-hire; in certain circumstances the author's name isn't listed, only the name of the series. Sometimes chapters of books are written as work-for-hire. A large herb book may have chapters on garden design, medicinal herbs, and culinary herbs, with each chapter written by a different person. A set fee is paid for the chapter or by the page. The fee can usually be negotiated, but once the contract is signed, it is set in stone.

My master's thesis in psychology was typed with carbon paper; my first book was written longhand and retyped by a secretary; later I sent out departmental reports after making photocopies; now my Macintosh and I are intimately bound together. I was hauled by my husband, kicking and screaming, to my first computer, but now my loyalty is unwavering. I may be preaching to the converted; if so, skip the next paragraph. If not, pay attention!

Use a computer to write for publication. Some contracts demand it, and all will shortly, unless you are a venerable and famous author with a long list of top-rated books who can dictate her own terms. The advantage is not just to the publisher but to you also. Change a word, a sentence, a paragraph, or a chapter.

Check your spelling; find synonyms. Rewrite and edit in a twentieth of the time it takes when typing. Writing becomes a pleasure because change is so easy.

If you feel that writing will be an important niche for you in your flower and herb business, educate yourself about the publishing business. In addition to the two books listed above, scan *Publishers Weekly* from time to time (order it from your library or find it in big city bookstores).

Join a local writers' workshop if one is available in your area or start one if there isn't. A writers' workshop provides regular meetings for published and would-be authors to support each other in the craft of writing and receive feedback on style and quality. One national writers' group is Garden Writers Association of America, whose regional and national meetings attract book and magazine writers, editors, publishers, and columnists.

The Authors Guild gives extremely valuable assistance on contract terms, negotiations, censorship, and other business matters of vital importance to writers. The guild, long an association just for published writers, now has an associate membership available for the unpublished writer. The newsletter alone is worth the price of membership if you're serious about writing.

Photography. If you don't like to write or feel your skills are subpar, perhaps you shine in photography. Take stills and slides of your best work or, with permission, of flower and herb gardens that you visit. Take stills for retail customers to promote custom orders; take slides for publication. Often the photographer makes as much money as the author of an article. Join with a friend who is better at writing and submit an article together; each of you will collect a fee for the work involved.

Illustration. Those with skills and talents in drawing can combine their botanical knowledge with artistic ability. One such person is Heather Lovett of Hopewell, New Jersey, who majored in printmaking at college and then did freelance illustrations for a variety of small publications. Her dream was to own an herb farm and raise plants for sale. Instead, she was encouraged by a local nursery to grow cut flowers and herbs for bouquets. Starting by selling wholesale, Heather soon realized that she was not growing the quantity to make that venture profitable and switched to retail cut flower sales, all the while continuing with her freelance illustration work and the garden column she writes monthly for the local newspaper. The cut flower business is seasonal, from May to mid-October where she lives, and she can devote the other months to her drawing and illustration projects. Her latest venture is to illustrate a technical gardening book, which she anticipates will take her about two years. Heather says that although she spends more hours on growing and gardening, the illustrating is more profitable.

PRESENTING A WORKSHOP OR DEMONSTRATION

When you have arranged to present a workshop or demonstration, arrive prepared. Ask for a letter of confirmation and check with the host about speaking conditions at least a month before the date. If possible, have the host provide a wearable (lapel) microphone; two tables, one to work on and one on which to lay out your materials; an extra light to illuminate your work table; a handy outlet or an extension cord (I go nowhere without my hot glue gun); a trash receptacle; a glass of water for dry-mouth when you're speaking and another for dipping your fingers when you dribble hot glue.

Here are some questions to ➛ **ask:**

• Who will help you carry materials in and out?

• Will there be a raised dais to make your presentation viewable from the back of the room? If not, bring a small wooden wine or fruit crate, or similar riser, to lift the height of the arrangement you are working on.

• How many people are expected? You need to bring enough materials to hand out.

• How do you get there? Go over the directions in advance with a state road map.

• What if you or your host must cancel because of bad weather? Set a time they can call you or you can call them if the roads are impassable. Will you be paid if the program is canceled?

- Who will introduce you? Mail him or her a short typed biography or PR statement.

If you are making several arrangements during the presentation, have materials for each in a separate box, and be sure to take enough. If you are making a wreath, bring a wreath hanger for putting it up and bring or request a standing easel with pad to serve as the background. Drape the easel in fabric of a contrasting or highlighting color to enhance the wreath.

Make a checklist of these other items:

- clippers
- glue gun and glue sticks (bring a spare glue gun incase one breaks down)
- extension cord
- pen and pencil
- cards and literature
- mailing list on clipboard with pen attached
- handouts
- a statement (bill) for the sponsor
- change for any sales you make at the program
- work apron with business name embroidered on it
- extra merchandise to sell
- a brief outline of what you want to say or topics to cover for each project
- your smile

Arrive in plenty of time to set out your materials, relax, and be gracious before the presentation. I always allow time to get lost, though rarely do I need it. Feeling rushed increases anxiety and you don't need that. Remember that moderate anxiety increases performance, so some stage fright is not only expected but a good thing. You will get more relaxed as you do more demonstrations. If something does go wrong, smile. Audiences are delighted to see that the expert has difficulties at times. Being able to improvise is more important than being perfect. Chef Julia Child once said that the sign of a good cook is knowing how to correct your mistakes. She never loses her sense of humor as she smears the frosting a little thicker on the thin side of the cake, evening out the lopsidedness.

In demonstrations, I also follow the Julia Child method of timing. Many lovely and original designs take thirty to sixty minutes or more to create, and if you showed the whole thing, the audience would be squirming in their chairs. To prevent this, I bring two or three versions of the design. For example, a design called a spiral topiary is made on a two-foot-tall wire frame, and the base alone uses two hundred stems of freshly cut tansy. I start with the frame, the wrapping wire, the pot, and the foam and show how to start the process, using all the mechanics and four clusters of flowers. Then, as Julia would remove a cake from the oven, I withdraw from an opaque plastic bag a completely wrapped base and show how to begin decorating the topiary, gluing on flowers with a hot glue gun. With great flourish I remove from a second bag a topiary tree that is almost complete. After gluing on the final touches, I take my bow; one and a half hours' work condensed into fifteen minutes.

If you need help with some clipping, trimming, or gluing, or just need an extra pair of hands, recruit a member of the audience to help. Those who are involved in some special way enjoy the program the most. After a few seconds of hesitation, there are always several hardy souls who volunteer. If you need help for several operations, change volunteers for each operation, getting more people involved.

At one demonstration I was promised a spot from which to hang a wreath for demonstration. When I arrived, there was no convenient spot on the platform to suspend the wreath. Some lovely woman held the wreath at eye level so that it could be decorated in full view of the audience. Now I take my own easel if I am showing a wreath, but I remember my savior.

Garden writers often lecture about their garden designs, bringing slides since the real thing is impossible to transport. The best lecturer I ever heard was Rosalind Creasy, author of *Cooking from the Garden* and several other fine books on gardening and cooking.

FROM IDEA TO PUBLISHED BOOK

I was extremely fortunate that Maggie Balitas, then the senior editor of the division of garden books at Rodale Press, called me and asked if I would be interested in writing a book for them. I had closed my psychology practice one week before, intending to devote full time to my Meadow Lark Flower & Herb Farm, but I hadn't as yet decided on my niche. Maggie had seen my designs both at open houses in my barn and at the Philadelphia Flower Show. I laughingly warned her that she had not yet seen a sample of my writing. She explained in the kindest possible terms that their excellent editors could clean up all the flaws in my writing; it was my design skills they were after. The result of our series of conversations led to the publication of *Flower Crafts*, and then three more books with Rodale. A brief summary of the steps to publication follows.

It began with Maggie's call to me about writing a book tentatively entitled *Flower Crafts from a Country Garden* and my

Her slides, which she takes herself, are spectacular in color, quality, and interest. But she never relies entirely on slides. She passes goodies around the audience for a more intimate show and tell and smell. I vividly remember the smell of her homemade paprika, which she passed around in a little cup to prove to the audience the value of making your own. Every member of the audience became a convert with one whiff.

return call to express my acceptance of the project. A discussion with Rodale about my vision of the book and their concurrence followed. I submitted my written proposal, including an outline and a list by name of all the designs to be submitted. Several meetings were held at Rodale by various committees approving my written proposal. I received a nineteen-page contract outlining the publisher's and the author's responsibilities and the financial terms. After going over the contract with my lawyer and doing some negotiating, I signed the contract and received the first part of my advance payment. I designed the projects and wrote the text. This was followed by ten photography sessions at Meadow Lark Flower & Herb Farm. The manuscript was submitted, and I received the last part of my advance. The manuscript was edited and queried and then returned to me. I submitted a rewrite, which underwent copyediting. The title page and other pages were designed, and the book was printed. Rodale put the book out for sale, and I promoted it heavily. I then started receiving royalties from the sales. ❧

CHAPTER SEVEN

Attitude Adjustment

As an artisan you may create delightful pieces with your flowers and herbs; your work may be fresh and original and your design well thought out. But you're in business; you still have to sell your wares, and *selling* may be the hardest part of the whole enterprise. Some growers are so enraptured with their materials and the product they create that they neglect the business side of the venture.

The first three to five years of business are the most difficult and the most likely period of failure. Much of the failure rate in the early years is due to undercapitalization—not having enough money to cover necessary start-up costs and negative cash flow until sales become brisk.

Another common reason for business failure in the early years, however, is attitude: having unrealistic expectations, being unable to assert oneself, taking rejection personally, ignoring customers' needs and requests, or being unwilling to look for solutions to problems.

As you read this chapter, see where you need an attitude adjustment to get your business off to a thriving start or to help it grow to its full potential.

BEING ASSERTIVE

Do you still harbor the idea you may have learned as a child that nice girls don't speak up? Remind yourself that in business, successful people speak up all the time to state what they need, what they want, and what they don't need or want. This behavior is called assertiveness. Throughout the book I have suggested that you must ∽ **ask for the help and information you need.**

In the middle of the summer, when new shipments of dried flowers and herbs arrive at the wholesalers, though last year's flowers may still be in stock, those who ask will receive the new crop. In many cases, those who don't ask for it will get tired, faded flowers.

Few reporters approach you pleading to write pieces on your fledgling business, but an editor's curiosity may be piqued by a press release you send to the paper. ∽ **Ask the editor to dispatch a photographer and reporter for a feature.**

∽ **Ask for deliveries when you need them,** rush if necessary, and check on any extra costs involved.

∽ **Ask in advance about cancellation fees for shows you want to enter** and make sure the arrangements are in writing.

Don't apologize for prices. When you've grown your own larkspur and consider all the sweat and dirt involved, you proudly offer bunches for sale at $4.75. When someone picks one up, shakes it heartily, asks if the flowers are real and whether the petals will drop, and says that's an outrageous price for larkspur, don't reach over the counter and throttle her. The dictum "don't complain, don't explain" applies here. The customer is entitled to her opinion and you are entitled to yours. Rather than feel put out, remember the times you went into a store and rejected merchandise because you thought it was too expensive. Smile nicely and suggest she look at some of your other lovely things.

Assertiveness involves saying no, firmly and politely, when the request interferes with your business goals.

Here are five good times to say no:

1. No, I don't give discounts to my friends and relatives. I have many of both and would have a hard time drawing the line. I have set my prices in a fair way to make a profit. I am in business and must make a profit to continue, otherwise my business fails. I give small or large gifts of my choosing to friends, relatives, and special customers. These include large bunches of fresh flowers when I have bumper crops, or several pressed-flower note cards or bags of potpourri with particularly large orders. (I confess that I make an exception for my children, who always have free rein to pick anything they want for their own use.)

2. No, I never reduce my speaking fee, even for worthwhile organizations and charities. Most audiences I speak to are doing a fund-raising project for some very good cause. Speaking to groups is part of my job, not a hobby. My charitable donations are decided on the basis of my personal views and interests and are private and separate from my work. I may donate a product of my own choosing to a charity if it fits in with my business purposes—that is, if I am approached by a good customer, if the cause is local and will list my business name as a donor, and will have my cards or literature available for distribution.

3. No, I don't give out my sources to other retailers for those special products that enhance my flower and herb work, that I have searched high and low for and now include as part of my line. The gift shop owner a mile from me who admired my unusual containers and wanted to order some just like them for her shop was told politely, and with regret, that it's our strict business policy not to reveal sources, but perhaps we could help her with some other ideas or information. Can you imagine one paint factory asking another for its paint formula because it was such good quality and they wanted to make some just like it?

4. No, I don't allow freelance professional photographers to take pictures of my products and garden unless they are willing to sign a release that they will give me a small credit line with the pic-

ture. One professional photographer disregarded my written permission statement and published my work in a magazine without attributing the work to me, but most are honorable.

5. No, I don't give lengthy free consultations on starting a flower and herb business. Though I did at one time, I found I was spending too many hours helping others and neglecting my own work. I always answer questions from customers about the flowers and herbs and construction of designs so that they can make their own, and I offer consultation on an hourly basis to anyone wanting my services on starting a business.

HANDLING REJECTION

Set up a charming booth at a crafts fair and watch the customers swarm to the jewelry booth across the way; bring your all-natural dried flower designs to a home and garden show and watch the customers walk by with armfuls of tissue paper flowers or painted silks; submit an article to the perfect magazine and never hear from the editors, or at best receive the standard rejection letter with your name spelled wrong. Giving up is easy; persistence in the face of rejection is hard.

If you've gotten as far as going to shows, it's probably because other people have admired your work and bought it. If you find yourself in a situation where buyers are spurning you, think of this as a data-gathering situation. Don't just guess why; try to answer these questions:

- Are people buying similar work from other vendors?
- Are people buying other crafts, but not flowers?
- Are people eschewing crafts for food?
- What is the price range of merchandise that is selling? What style seems popular? Is it contemporary and you have country or vice versa?
- In a commercial show, talk to the administration. Ask how the sales compare with those of previous years.
- Talk to other vendors. How do their sales compare with those of previous years?

- If you have a shop, do you get many repeat customers or do you waste financial resources by having to constantly recruit new ones?
- How did new customers hear about you?

Now analyze your data and observations carefully, and draw your conclusions.

I once took a booth at a popular one-day crafts show. That day the temperature hovered around ninety-seven degrees with humidity also in the nineties. As a newcomer to the show, I was assigned a space in a sunny field. I had one small umbrella for protection, but my customers were left to swelter on their own. My direct competition had a booth of high-quality dried flower arrangements; this vendor had been there for years and was now ensconced beneath the old shade trees. Guess who got the lion's share of business that day?

In a similar situation, remind yourself it takes several years of building up a clientele and word-of-mouth publicity before people start looking for you. I decided not to compete at that show in future years; I would only do shows where I could have a protected location. In the shows where I choose to compete, I have watched my sales grow each year until now I am the competition for newcomers.

Many times the only way you will be able to tell if a venue works for you is to take the risk and try it. If you can keep your traveling expenses low and are prepared to handle a small loss if necessary, try to learn why an unsuccessful venue isn't for you. Compare it with other shows where you are successful and try to tease out the critical elements.

Customers may reject certain styles while admiring others that you produce. Again, collect data. Price is always one consideration but may not be the most important. With dried materials, fragility is a common reason why customers at a large flower show don't buy. Arrangements are difficult to ship, to carry around all day, to take home on the plane, or to get in the overhead compartment of a tour bus. An avant-garde style may be admired by other professionals but may not be a popular purchase with your clientele. Your designs might be excellent, but your choice of colors may not work in most homes. If possible, eavesdrop on conversations between two women shopping together; they'll tell each other what they won't tell you.

Sometimes standards and designs slip; your wares get old and tired looking and you lose your design energy. One way of testing yourself is by entering shows that require jurying. A jury of craftspeople and show organizers look at four or five samples of your work, either slides or the actual objects, and determine whether you qualify for the show. The decision of the jury is final; there is usually no appeal. A good jury for a nonprofit organization will make brief comments that will help you learn. If you fail the selection process, you can enter again the next year, learning from the comments how to better your work and make it appropriate for that particular show.

REFRESHING YOUR CREATIVITY

At some point most artisans wonder whether they will run out of fresh ideas for designs. One designer I know pictures creativity as a huge pot from which she keeps dipping. She is certain that eventually she will reach the bottom of the pot and run out of ideas, a horrifying notion. Instead, think of creativity as a great stream that continues to flow; the artisan dips a ladle in at any part of the stream and is refreshed by its cool waters.

Here are a dozen ways to refresh yourself when you feel dry:

1. Page through your old flower and herb books, enjoying the photos.

2. Visit a good library. If you live near a big city that has a horticultural society with a public library, head there. Commune with the collection of flower and herb books and trade magazines.

3. Go to a bookstore that carries an extensive selection of magazines; purchase a few foreign home and garden magazines. Leaf through the latest shelter magazines to see what's new in home decor.

4. Go to a juried crafts show and inspect crafts not in your medium. Pay attention to the ceramics, the glass, the paper, the metal, and the wood designs.

5. Go to a fabulous antique show and analyze artifacts, ephemera, and jewelry. Look at the materials the old artisans used in the designs.

6. Go to a professional workshop or presentation. They are given at large gift shows, state florist conventions, and most national and local crafts shows. Even if you don't belong to a craftsmen's guild, ∿ **ask a friend to invite you as a guest when an interesting speaker will present a program.**

7. Sign up for a crafts class in some other medium. One that inspired me was on Japanese packaging given at the Cooper Hewitt Museum in New York by basketmaker Nancy Moore Bess. It sounds rather far afield from flower and herbal crafts, but I learned some techniques and got some ideas that were highly translatable to my own work.

8. Go to a museum of art, natural history, crafts, ethnic traditions, or folk art; almost any collection or compilation can inspire. Again, look at materials, styles, and designs.

9. Wander along the most upscale retail street of any big city or some wealthier towns and suburbs. Window-shop at fine crafts galleries and flower shops, looking not at the merchandise but at the displays.

10. Give yourself quiet time away from your materials to try out different designs in your mind. Set yourself a problem, like how to incorporate pansies into a design or magnolia into a Christmas wreath, or brainstorm a set of ideas.

11. Browse at the top wholesale gift shows. Look at the newest containers and products. These will often inspire a use.

12. Saunter through flea markets, looking at old containers and products. These may suggest styles and solutions. It was when I saw a dealer selling old watch pieces and parts at a very low cost that I designed a line of thyme wreaths to incorporate the parts. I had the thyme, but not the idea, until I saw the lovely enamel watch faces and itched to use them.

When I write about observing, checking, and reading, I am definitely not suggesting copying someone else's work, nor am I suggesting putting pressure on yourself to come up with an idea. Just flow free and enjoy yourself. The payoff for you can be direct, as in my thyme example, or indirect, buried in your subconscious to reappear as a new idea.

KEEPING CURRENT
Even if your flower niche is a historical or traditional one, be aware of trends in materials and design. Whether you want to add another line or another color combination, small changes to indicate you are up-to-date are appreciated by customers.

Trends in design filter down from big city to small town. It was five years after I first noticed the quantities of sunflowers in the wholesale markets that a friend from Orwigsburg suggested to me that sunflowers were getting popular and I might want to carry some.

Trends in flower design also travel from Tokyo, Paris, London, Brussels, and Amsterdam. If you are fortunate enough to travel abroad on vacation, you will surely want to see what the best shops in foreign cities are carrying. Barring that, foreign home decorating magazines reveal the latest trends. Magazines have a much shorter lead time from conception to print than books, so they are more up to the minute. Buy magazines like *Elle Decoration* in any of its foreign language editions or *Marie Claire Idées*. You needn't speak or read the language to connect with the glossy color photos. Here is a case where a picture is definitely worth a thousand words. Note that almost every room depicted, and many of the advertisements, use flower designs to enhance the look. You can easily bypass them if you're not specifically looking for them. But they are often created by the premier designers in the country. Compare your work with the best you see, using your most critical eye. Make adjustments as necessary.

THINKING POSITIVE
Words have power, and labels foster conclusions. If, after five years, an item that you started with is still selling well, call it your

"classic line" rather than thinking of it as "the same old thing." What a difference it makes to be selling something "funky," rather than something "weird." Your "upscale" line certainly sounds more welcoming than your "expensive" line. "Cheap" is not a synonym for "competitively priced." Learning to set a positive tone in your speech also promotes a positive tone in your thinking and changes the way you perceive your work. Monitor your speech and labeling patterns to see what effect they are having on your promotional efforts.

In the computer field when some design element goes awry, creative salespeople indicate that it's not a bug, it's a feature, and proceed to explain how the feature can be incorporated to the user's benefit.

In my own design work, I discovered how "bugs" can become "features." My inventory of any one type of container is modest, as I prefer to make one-of-a-kind pieces. In my summer garden, I have hundreds of varieties of flowers and herbs, but no huge quantities of any one variety. I was once asked to make thirty-five centerpieces for a party on short notice, and having no time to order, I started of necessity to mix and match the designs. I used the same color scheme and many of the same elements, but each centerpiece was slightly different. I found, to my astonishment, that I greatly preferred the custom look of a party room where flowers coordinated but weren't identical. Now I explain to the customer what my vision is, and I have never had a complaint. In fact, customers seem to prefer this custom feature. Imagine if I confessed that I had to improvise because I didn't have enough stock.

ACTING LIKE A PROFESSIONAL

If you are in business, even part-time, you must assume a professional attitude if you want people to take you seriously. If you underprice your wares or overdo your expenses, you will soon lose enough money to make business nonviable. Check yourself on the following amateur-professional indices and see where you stand.

A enters a crafts show. Earns a pocketful of jingle. Shops the show. Buys wonderful crafts from other vendors. Comes home with nothing to deposit.

P enters a crafts show. Earns a pocketful of jingle. Returns home and deposits all the money in the bank, entering sales in an accounts register.

A enters a show. Buys meals and coffee at show food stand. Has dinner in best restaurant in town. Stays in a fine hotel closest to the show. Spends three-quarters of the profits on expenses.

P brown-bags her lunch and snacks. Brings thermos. Stays with friends or at an inexpensive motel. Has dinner at an ethnic restaurant, cheap but good.

A buys all supplies at retail. Pays sales tax. Doesn't collect state sales tax even though applicable.

P goes to wholesale markets and distributors to buy supplies. Doesn't pay sales tax. Collects sales tax and makes required returns to the state.

A goes to a wholesale show for containers. Buys everything that looks wonderful.

P shops the show carefully. Has a budget to spend and a marketing list. Gets overview first. Picks up literature. Makes notes. Then goes back to buy. Asks for terms. Takes credit sheet with her.

A has basement full of old supplies—last year's overruns and mistakes. Always works with the newest purchases.

P keeps track of inventory. Finds ways to use old supplies. Sprays gold, donates, knows when refurbishing costs too much, composts the leftovers.

A performs all tasks herself, even when her sales are growing.

P hires others part- or full-time to do some less preferred and less skilled jobs and jobs she is less proficient at. Hires reps and bookkeeper while she continues to design. Or hires an assistant designer while she sells. Uses contract services where possible to avoid the expense and time of figuring payroll.

A acts embarrassed when people praise her work. Says, "It really isn't that original" or "I'm really only a beginner."

P smiles and says, "Thank you, that's my latest design. I'm thrilled you picked it out. Here, have a closer look."

CHAPTER EIGHT

Public Relations, Promotion, and Advertising

A woman dressed in black velvet enters a glittering holiday party and surveys the crowd. In her antique beaded purse are her freshly printed business cards and a small pad and pencil. She heads toward a group of chatting women, knowing the question that will inevitably arise: "What have you been up to lately?" Out come the cards, accompanied by a riveting but brief account of her new flower and herb crafts business.

Swirling on to the next group, the woman falls into conversation with a writer, the local stringer for an out-of town paper. After commenting on the writer's latest article, the woman offers her interesting news, and cards change hands.

"Working the room" is a time-honored strategy used to accomplish specific goals. Sometimes a goal is deliberately formed in advance: I will talk to whatever accountants are present and see what interest they show in a new small business customer. Sometimes the goals are vague and general: While I'm having a good time at the party I'll also see if I can learn something to help my business now or to promote my business later. People who have been in business for years automatically work the room. If you've ever been an officer or committee chairperson for a nonprofit organization, you are probably used to walking into a large event and looking for contacts or potential donors who will help your worthy cause and save you a few phone calls. Now the worthy cause is you, and you must promote your business where you can, not to the exclusion of all other conversation, but in a way that initiates the interaction, to be followed up another time—thus the pad and paper to make a note to yourself regarding the follow-up.

WHAT ARE YOU TRYING TO SELL?

Examine your business. Think of your niche and decide whether you are trying to sell primarily services or primarily goods? If your plan is to sell to corporate clients, you are providing a service, taking care of all the office decorations, staying within the agreed-upon budget, and delivering appropriate gifts to the client's customers. Your client probably won't care whether you deliver a manzanita wreath with curly willow and oak leaves or a freeze-dried rose ring with rosemary as long as the recipient is happy. So when you place your ad in the chamber of commerce newsletter, emphasize the service aspect of your work, not the product; emphasize how you can simplify corporate gift giving and decoration.

Perhaps you have a new line of homemade whole flower potpourri. Unlike most products on the market, it has no fillers, includes whole roses, dahlias, and peonies, and is meant for show, not to hide in a jar. It's the perfect gift when the buyer isn't sure about the size or color preferences. You may define your goal as selling a certain quantity of this potpourri in a specific period of time. Here you are selling a product to engender a sense of well-being, friendship, comfort, stylishness, love of nature, and creativity.

Gonnie McClung Siegel, in the book *How to Advertise and Promote Your Small Business*, quotes from an SBA course on administration management that "people don't buy things, they buy goods that satisfy wants." The SBA reports seven wants:

1. Convenience and comfort
2. Love or friendship
3. Security
4. Social approval or status
5. Life, health, and well-being
6. Profit, savings, or economy
7. Stylishness

In the flower and herb business, I would add two more:

8. Love of nature and spirituality
9. Creativity

People will buy from you because dried flowers and herbs are *stylish*. Examine the finest shelter magazines. No room is photographed without some adornment of natural materials—a bowl of lemons, a stand of bare twigs in an elegant urn, an herbal topiary, a crystal vase of flowers, a dried flower swag draping a window, or a plant. Some are fresh; some are silk; many are dried and preserved.

Surrounded by natural materials, people have a feeling of *well-being*. Note how on fire escapes in the poorest sections of town there are often containers filled with growing things. Plants struggle for survival in unexpected places: the dark reaches of the windowsill at the tire store or an interior cubicle among the sea of work stations on the computer floor of a large business.

Decorating a home with dried flowers and herbs promotes *approval* from others for the warmth and naturalness of the home.

The *convenience* of dried materials is that they needn't be replaced as often as fresh, and once in position, they don't need watering, fertilizing, or repotting. They are perfect for a busy life or a vacation home.

When you provide workshops or demonstrations, when you sell bunches and containers for people to design their own things, you are offering the opportunity to fulfill *creative needs*.

In your advertising, highlight the product or service you wish to sell and pitch it to a need that the customer wants to satisfy. You will have a match made in heaven.

SELLING THE FANTASY

When you buy Bordeaux Blush cheek color, even though you have eleven partially used pots of color in your dressing table drawer, you are buying into the Cinderella fantasy that with a swish of the magic wand, you will suddenly become enchantingly beautiful and run off with the prince.

When you create a wisteria wreath crowned with colorful native wildflowers, the product is only part of the story. A fantasy accompanies all of your wares. The customer's home will be more alive and enchanting. She and her friends can feel that she is up on the latest trends, returning to the natural, the native, and the handcrafted.

As an artisan creating with natural materials, you have a distinct advantage over other vendors. Part of what you are selling is the connection between you and the buyer. You as an individual design and create the product for the customer to enjoy in her home or office. Perhaps you are growing or collecting part of the materials you are using. From seed to centerpiece, the creative chain is exposed for all to follow. As you explain in person or in writing on a hangtag, the customer feels drawn to your work as she can never feel to a product manufactured on an impersonal assembly line.

And because you are working with plant materials, the buyer feels a connection to the earth, a craving felt at some level by all humans. One of the basic needs in life is to be in tune with nature. For survival of the species, all people had to learn to appreciate and respect the basic elements of earth, air, fire, and water. They had to observe the changing seasons and learn how to protect themselves from severe changes by sheltering themselves, how to hunt or gather food, and how to preserve or store it for the lean times.

We still observe the changing of the seasons in our own ways. The fall ritual of buying new school clothes and school supplies is but one. The first child in spring who marches into school with a fistful of early tulips or sprig of azalea is cooed over by the teacher and all the other kids know it. My mother's presummer, pre-air-conditioning ritual was to roll up and store the wool rugs and replace them with sisal and to slipcover the furniture in pastel shades. Spring cleaning was a massive effort involving the whole family. The first whiff of burning leaves in the fall air meant riding out to our "bittersweet man" parked by the side of Route 23 for our annual fix of tangerine and golden berries. Long before I was in the flower business, I left standing instructions with the florist that if anyone ever ordered flowers for me, the arrangement was to include only seasonal materials, no mums in the spring, no tulips in the fall. Many homemakers change their flower decor with the seasons.

In promoting your sales, tap into the fantasies. Observe the changing seasons in your designs and your advertising. Make the connection to the growth and preservation of the natural materials. You know how a whiff of floral or herbal scents from fresh or dried materials can instantaneously conjure memories of days long past.

Let your customers know something about you and your own connections to the materials you are working with. If you don't plant or gather the materials yourself, define yourself as an artisan and emphasize what is unique about you and your work. This is no time for false humility.

There's also the fantasy about your lifestyle as a designer of flower and herb crafts. Most of us got into the business after another career. People are fascinated by transition stories: Where did you come from and how did you get where you are? Encourage questions that will make the customer more knowledgeable and build a relationship.

YOUR ADVERTISING BUDGET

As with every phase of your business, you should have an idea of what you will spend yearly for advertising and promotion. Your budget will depend on the nature of your business as well as on how much you have in the bank. If you sell solely through retail crafts and flower shows, you can assume that the promoter will take care of the advertising. One of the factors in deciding whether to do a show is the extent to which the promoter advertises. Your only need might be to send a mailing to previous customers likely to attend that show to extend a personal invitation to visit your booth.

Perhaps the next step in your business development will be to have a holiday open house or reception at your workshop. You will be advertising just for that event, by both direct mail and media advertising.

If your shop is open April through Christmas, your advertising year will also be predetermined. Do you want an annual Spring Fling when you fling open your doors each year to celebrate the new growing season and the return of your customers? Your reopening should be well advertised so that previous customers will remember you.

I am avoiding specific figures and percentages of your gross income to spend on this budget item for two reasons. First, you must advertise heavily your first year before you have any idea what your sales figures will be. And second, as hard as it is to do, it is more important to advertise when business is bad than when your shop is well established. When word of mouth has pinpointed your store as the place to shop for home and gifts and the place to browse quietly for an afternoon pick-me-up, media advertising becomes less crucial to your existence.

To budget, you must know the prices for all of the media, including any special deals for quantity ads, reinsertions, or a specific number of days. Perhaps your favorite newspaper charges full price for one insertion of a display ad, 25 percent off the next day, and 50 percent off the third day. ⌒ **Ask what the terms are before you plan your budget.** A paper may offer a large discount on repeated advertising on weekly, biweekly, or monthly terms on a space-available basis. That means that although you save money, you will have no say on where in the paper your ad will appear or when. It might appear on the obituary page rather than in the home section. Find out rates for radio spots and TV ads on local stations (the latter probably to file away under "I really learned something today") and spot ads on the local weather and program channels on your cable service.

Read Small Business Administration publications on advertising for overall media principles.

The Classifieds

The classifieds are the cheapest of the print ads, and I use them for end-of-year sales. My year comes to an end in spring when I clear out last year's flowers to make way for the new crop. For many shops, the year ends after Christmas. I slash prices on dried flower bunches and ready-made items that I don't want to hold for the next year and on some damaged and distressed goods. I do a thorough spring cleaning. At 35 to 75 percent off the original price, crafters are happy to pick up bargains. I am competing with other yard and garage sales in my prices, so I must rely on inexpensive advertising for the event.

I announce workshops at the Meadow Lark first by newsletter to my loyal customers and then on the shop bulletin board. Some classes fill up immediately, but I also use classifieds to advertise those workshops that have a few places left. My goal is to fill each class at the lowest possible cost.

Local Advertising Tabloids

An all-ad paper might seem like a sleazy place to display your carefully constructed advertisement. But if *you* search the paper weekly for sales, bargains, auctions, and goodies, and hear that your friends and neighbors do the same, give it a try. The rates will probably be lower than your newspaper's, and the publisher may offer a discount for advertising in several papers within driving range.

I was amazed to find that the paper I sneered at gave me a better return both per dollar and in absolute volume than my respectable county newspaper. I have become a true believer in trying various possibilities, as long as you follow up with research.

The Yellow Pages

Before my days in the flower business, I routinely asked new clients in my psychology practice how they had gotten my name; I was not surprised by referrals from doctors and social service agencies and word of mouth from a friend or family member, but the yellow pages? Nearly a quarter of my clients were self-referrals who found my name in the yellow pages of the county phone book and said things like "You were the only woman" or "I knew your name through the PTA."

Deciding where to shop for dried flowers and herbs is a less weighty decision than choosing a therapist, and the yellow pages prove to be an excellent way to let people know that you have a serious business established.

Neighborhood and Ethnic Newspapers

These specialty newspapers may be of value to you. They are usually weekly, with distribution Thursday or Friday in time for weekend sales. The rates are relatively low; the audience is geographically or ethnically determined; and the subscribers are often loyal to the advertisers. Some neighborhood weeklies give extended editorial and news coverage to their advertisers. When you hope to get a press release printed, you will often get a favorable response if you are an advertiser.

Radio

Check rates, including those for repeats, and discuss who would be reading the copy. How does your voice sound recorded? If you sound charming, friendly, and natural, by all means record your own spots. Despite twenty-five years of living in the coal region of Pennsylvania, my Philadelphia accent still comes dripping through, and I don't like the sound. I prefer to have a professional record my spots.

Is there an appropriate radio program in your area whose demographics match that of your customers? My customers are 98 percent women, between the ages of twenty-five and sixty. We have two stations in town, both at the moment with an unsettling mix of rock and hate talk. "Golden oldies" means from 1980 to 1985. How I long for someone to produce a local garden show where I could try out a series of spots.

Newspapers

There may be several newspapers that cover your shopping area. Cost is an obvious consideration. Check whether there are special days of saturation coverage or special regional sections that might target audiences closer to home. Decide which section of the paper would be best for you; the paper's ad rep can help you with this. The home section gives me the best coverage. Usually the sales rep can't promise a specific site; too many people want to be next to "Dear Abby." She will be able to place your ad in the section you request, however.

Despite your best guess on which paper might be read by more of your customers, there is only one way to tell if your advertising is drawing people to your shop. Research!

DIRECT MAIL

Postage and paper are expensive and getting more so every day, but with direct mail you advertise only to people of your own selection. Start developing your mailing list even before you open your doors. For me that means collecting names of people who have expressed a direct interest in my product by buying something or making a personal request to be put on the list. This is not a scattershot approach. I don't buy names or even use the lists that would be available to me by hook or by crook from other community organizations. I take my mailing list tablet to every lecture I give and every show I attend.

With large shows like the Philadelphia or New York Flower Show, I keep the list out of sight. I don't collect autographs, but the names of genuine prospects—people who buy at the show or people who feel that a three-hour drive to my barn is an adventure. The qualifying goes something like this:

"Do you have a mailing list?" the customer asks.

"Yes," I say with a welcoming smile. "Where do you live?"

"Short Hills, New Jersey."

"That's about two hours, an easy drive on Route 78."

"I hate to drive," she says.

I smile and shrug my shoulders. "Well, I hope to see you here again next year." I don't produce the list. Then a second customer approaches and asks me about my mailing list.

"Oh, driving two hours is nothing for me," she says. "I love to take jaunts in the summer."

"We'd love to see you," I say. "Here is my sign-up sheet for the mailing list."

My mailing list now includes about thirty-five hundred names from all over the country. About 90 percent of those on the mailing list live within a two-hour drive of my shop. The rest are people who have bought my books and have written to me, people who buy from me at large shows, friends and family of local residents who are brought to the barn when they visit Pennsylvania, audiences from programs I do farther afield, and personal friends. I add the name and address of anyone who thinks I'm the phone encyclopedia, calling to ask how to dry Valentine roses, how to stabilize topiaries for wedding centerpieces, and when to pick their hydrangeas.

The cost per unit (design time plus paper plus labor to print and affix labels plus postage) is high, but the cost per sale is low because of the excellent return rate. Many books on the subject say that for small businesses, direct mail with a good list gives the best return of any form of advertising, and for me this is definitely so.

As you collect names I urge you to put the list in a computer. You will then be able to print out mailing labels in short order. A process that takes about an hour for me on my slow old Mac would take about five days by hand if anyone could bear to do the task. A computer enables you to sort the list by zip code, a necessity if you want to mail bulk rate, or by any other notation you add to the hidden field. You can note at which crafts show you gathered the names, for example, and send personal postcards to that select list before the next show in that locale.

The computer is also my main design source for my newsletter. Although untrained in graphic design, I am able to produce a professional-looking piece. My daughter Jenny designed my first newsletter on her computer, then entered law school and got too busy with her own work to continue. I repeatedly use her format and headings, and by a combination of clip art and old-style cut and paste with output from my word processor program and laser printer, I am on my eighth edition of the newsletter. I promise myself that one of these days I'll buy the best graphics program available and set aside the time to learn to use it.

If you have a shop, use direct mail to announce sales and special events in addition to your regular media advertising. Since my business is open only for special events and workshops, and on a call-ahead basis, my media advertising is timed to the special events, but my newsletters go out twice a year to my complete mailing list. I use custom postcards as reminders between newsletters.

For both postcards and newsletters, I select paper of a color, quality, and texture that stands out above the average. The cards are designed to be bigger than the standard size, yet not go over the lowest postal rate. Check sizes with the post office when you are ready to design. Also check with your printer on the most economical cut size for the paper you are selecting. The mail piece must say to the recipient, this is too interesting to throw away before reading. Additional costs for better paper run about $30, a cost I feel is well justified when people remark to me about the elegance of my mailings. If I were mailing more frequently, I might have to reduce the costs of each, but for now I get away with it. When I am mailing first class, I select my stamps for their subject matter and artistic elegance. The Orwigsburg postmaster, knowing of my interest, always alerts me when new flower designs are being issued.

If you are mailing a small number of cards, perhaps under two hundred, you may choose to print them yourself if your laser printer can handle card stock. Print several to a page and cut them with a paper cutter afterward.

My first newsletter was on white stock printed in forest green ink. I hand painted it while watching TV. For most of the five hundred issued, I merely washed pink watercolor over one old rose illustration. For about fifty, going to VIPs, I painted everything in sight. Fortunately, I had the summer Olympics to keep me glued to the set. Between Wimbledon Tennis Finals, the Gulf War, the Clarence Thomas hearings, and other riveting events, I've managed to paint a lot of newsletters. Now thirty-five hundred is more than I can bear, so I paint only VIP mailings, and occasionally splurge with a second color ink in my print order.

Postal Rates

Rates keep changing, so check on the current price. As I write this, a first-class letter is 32 cents, and a postcard is 20 cents. Bulk mail varies from 14.2 cents to 22.6 cents per piece. The cheapest rate will probably not apply to you, as it involves bar coding and five plus four zip coding. In order to send bulk mail, you must bundle according to zip code and pay an application fee of $80 and a yearly mailing permit fee of $80. ∾ **Ask your printer to let you use his mailing permit.** If you bundle the mail, he probably won't charge you for the use. My post office said this is a legitimate practice. Printers will also sort and bundle according to zip code for a fee per piece and will mail out using their permits. Decide in advance of printing how you will approach a third-class permit, because the stamp is printed at *the same time* as your advertising copy. Bulk mail is slower, but if mail is going locally, that shouldn't make much difference. In any case, allow for delays.

Remember that if you persist in mailing third-class, you will get no returns of undeliverable mail and no forwarding addresses. Each year perhaps 1 to 3 percent of the people on your list will move, divorce, or die. In five years, over 10 percent of your list will be inaccurate. What a waste! You must have a way of cleaning up the list periodically to change addresses and remove names. My solution to the expense versus accuracy dilemma is this: My newsletters go out third-class, and once a year I mail a postcard reminder for a Holiday Open House first-class. The postcard rate is almost as cheap as a third-class letter. All the address changes and returns are entered into my computer, and I have a relatively clean list for another year.

The newsletter is entitled "From the Farm" and is printed on an 8½-by-14-inch two-fold mailer without envelope. It includes the following information:

- Descriptions of classes and registration instructions
- Open house weekends and special events
- Yearly Barn Sale
- Brief articles on such subjects as new flowers for drying, care tips for dried flowers, and when to pick hydrangeas for drying
- A calendar of my public appearances beyond home base. (This tells customers where and when to find me speaking, demonstrating, and selling, and suggests the idea that I am available to other groups.)
- Coupons for special items
- A map and directions to Meadow Lark Flower & Herb Farm and the hours we're open
- Help wanted ads as necessary

YOUR MARKETING REACH

Define your marketing area in order to better concentrate your resources. Check your mailing list to see where most of your current customers live. If your work is of excellent quality, fresh, and appealing, you should have no trouble drawing people from at least thirty miles away. If you give customers a good reason for buying from you, they will probably take an hour's drive to see your work. If you have a special ambience—your shop is in the country, a tourist town, a university town, or a historic district—folks will have a good reason to take a longer ride.

If you sell in a tourist area, where new people are continually coming and going, set a goal to gain recognition for your workshop and garden as a prime tourist sight. Find out which organization is responsible for tourist promotion and how it operates; consider joining it. Print promotional pieces that fit in the racks at every tourist stop, hotel, and motel. Research how to get your pieces distributed and consider whether it is more efficient and cheaper in the long run to do it yourself or to distribute as part of the organization.

Given your particular budget to spend on publicity and advertising, allocate your expenditures in the locales guaranteed to produce the best results. For example, I never buy advertising in the Philadelphia media, which is ninety-five miles away, but I gladly spend the money for a first-class stamp to invite all those people on my mailing list to come to workshops and special events. I compile the names initially while doing shows away from home. Always surprised and delighted when they appear, I try to be especially attentive to their needs. People who travel a distance can be counted on to take their time shopping, making the trip worthwhile for themselves and for me. I direct them to a nice little restaurant for lunch or tea and, if I have help in the shop, occasionally invite a guest from afar to tour my farmhouse.

When you are going away from home base to exhibit at a crafts or flower show, scan your mailing list for people who live in that area and send them a special card of invitation. Some big shows have preprinted announcements giving dates and times of the show. You simply fill in your name and booth number, and scrawl a personal note in a different color ink: "Hope to see you, Ellen." Even more appealing are personalized cards you produce yourself in small quantities on your computer.

It is lovely to have a feature article written about you in the *San Francisco Chronicle*, but if you sell in Shaker Heights, Ohio, the article will not provide much of a draw to your retail shop or to your studio open house. You can, however, use distant publicity about yourself in several ways, to get more immediately useful publicity. Clip and frame important articles and display them prominently at crafts and flower shows; incorporate quotations from articles about your work in your own brochures; send articles about yourself to hometown papers, which may be pleased to include a press release such as "Women in the News: Article about Local Woman Appears in the *San Francisco Chronicle*." Invariably, people are more impressed when you achieve recognition at a distance than they are when you receive the same accolades closer to home.

PROMOTION AND PUBLICITY

Paid advertisement is necessary but expensive, and when you need it most, at the start-up of your business, you may feel least able to afford it. So seek opportunities to promote your business apart from purchased media space. Publicity is not a substitute for paid advertising, but it repeats the message and enhances awareness of you and your craft.

Though publicity is often free, you may have little control over it. Media may accept for free publication or free air time only a small portion of what you send in, and they can change it as they wish. If a paper prints your schedule of classes in its adult education section, think of it as a bonus. They may choose to print only part of the schedule or, if this month's list is too long, may drop you in favor of someone else. You must also have a publicity method you can count on absolutely, and if your news release is published, be grateful for the repetition of information. Some of the best opportunities for publicity will be those you create yourself or plan for in advance.

A quarter to as much as half of your time each week should be spent on marketing your wares. This includes promotion. Planning for your publicity and advertising campaigns starts before you plant your first seed or order your first flowers.

First, think of where you live and what opportunities are available there. I can hear the huge sighs from those who live in rural areas or small towns where there seems to be nothing. Think again.

It is often easier to arrange for publicity in less populated areas. Brainstorm opportunities with friends and family. Here are some starting points:

1. Write press releases about all upcoming newsworthy events—an opening, workshops, house tours, out-of-town shows and talks, and appearances on radio and TV. Distribute them to newspapers, including those city papers that have special editions covering news in your town. Send them to electronic media that have community bulletin boards in your marketing area.

2. Write and distribute press releases about all past events, awards, offices in professional organizations, and public appearances to such columns as "People in the News," "Business Briefs," or "Talk of the Town." Scan business columns and look for columnists who write about sales trends. Perhaps your hook will be how your business survived despite bad weather this winter by sending out a special mailing offer to gift wrap and deliver all gifts. Instead of "record snows devastate retail sales," offer "local artisan creates sales during record snows." Articles on coping with disasters are generally popular.

3. Write news in the appropriate format for your college alumni bulletin, your high school reunion booklet, the newsletter at your day job, and other organizations that you belong to, both local and national, like the Rotary, the chamber of commerce, and the AAUW. Editors of newsletters all over the country have space to fill on a regular basis; why shouldn't it include news about you?

4. If you are now living and working far from your hometown, remember that your hometown media will often print hometown-girl-makes-good-in-the-big-city articles. A feature piece with photographs may lead to a few calls and mail-order sales; more important, you can use the clippings to produce more interest and recognition.

5. Search for network and cable TV and radio talk shows in your area that feature personalities who are doing interesting things or who are dedicated to gardening, flowers, and herbs. Lis-

ten to or watch the show, then contact the producer or host directly. Send written materials about yourself, then follow up within a week with a phone call referring to the publicity package or press kit that you sent. Discuss how you could fit into the format of the show.

6. Donate one "scholarship" to a workshop you will be giving to a charity auction. Describe the workshop in arresting terms; give the date and value. Make sure that the description and date will be printed in the charity booklet and that your full workshop schedule can be available to other attendees. Those who don't enter the winning bid might still call to enroll for a workshop. If you feel the audience would be an excellent opportunity for you, offer the charity an extra 10 percent rebate for every attendee who signs up that night.

7. Join local organizations that foster business or crafts in your locality, such as a chapter of the state craftsmen's guild, the downtown business association, or the tourist promotion agency. Your name and the name of your business will be included in all their publicity and their membership directory. If the organization advertises, rates for joint ads are often cheaper than the rate for advertising alone. Many organizations make it a special point to patronize their own members for goods and services. Offer to host a meeting of the organization at your place of business; offer light refreshments, including herbal baked goods.

8. If you are lucky enough to have an arts center in your community, become an active member. There will be many times when their needs will coincide with your own. When the arts center wants to decorate for Christmas or another special event, offer to design and decorate one of the rooms that will be in use for the whole holiday season. Leave plenty of cards and brochures for admirers to pick up.

9. Get involved in community action and join or chair a committee that is especially relevant to the image or needs of your business. Pay attention to historic preservation, tree plantings, and park or street beautification. Offer your expertise, resources, and ability

to roll up your sleeves and get dirty. Anything that makes the community more livable also aids the business community, and that includes you.

10. Many public libraries have display cases or areas where they show crafts of local artisans. If libraries in your area provide such an opportunity, ➤ **ask how you can participate.** If no display is available, ➤ **ask how you can create such a space.**

11. If you own a shop, create a window display of historical or educational value. Feature a collection of old herbals, botanical books and prints with samples of the dried materials, apothecary jars with medicinal herbs, a display of dried roses, and old vases with rose motifs. Work with a nearby antique shop and arrange to borrow some items in exchange for credit in your display window. Notify the local media of the display. Make this another opportunity for press releases. Request that a photographer be sent to capture the images.

12. Write letters to the editor on flower- and herb-related matters. When a spring photo appeared in the local newspaper mislabeling clouds of ethereal blossoms, I wrote to identify the trees and to give credit to the young woman who had organized the tree planting at the town square. My name and business appeared in small letters at the bottom of the letter. After it was published many people mentioned seeing the letter.

13. Using clip art, computer-generated art, your own skills, or those you can buy inexpensively, design attractive posters that advertise special events. Display these around town on community bulletin boards and wherever acceptable to the space owner. If you have your posters professionally printed, provide camera-ready artwork and layout to reduce cost. Choose paper that will make a readable background yet set your poster apart from others. Save on printing costs by washing areas of the poster with watercolor paints. This process can be done quickly and inexpensively during the course of an evening in front of the TV. Use appropriate computer bulletin boards to announce your special events.

14. Some smaller papers have year-end supplements, business

reviews, home and garden supplements, or bridal sections. They are offered as a way for the paper to sell special advertising, and they offer two possibilities for you. ⌒ **Ask whether the paper writes feature articles about advertisers** (many do) and whether the article would include a photograph. Will the paper accept an article by you about a relevant topic and give you and your business credit? You might suggest an article on the best flowers and herbs to grow for drying for a garden supplement, or how to make a floral headpiece for a bridal supplement. Though you probably won't get paid for this kind of piece, your business gets a mention.

15. With everything you achieve, always look for at least three more opportunities for promotion and publicity.

I was invited to appear on the "Plant Doctor" TV show to demonstrate how to arrange flowers from the garden. The host announced my upcoming open house on the air (after I asked) and he promoted my new book. I sent a news release about my appearance on TV to the local paper, which printed it. That one appearance resulted in three promotional opportunities.

PRESS RELEASES

Your publicity will be tied to some extent to your method of sales. If you are selling wholesale through galleries or retail through crafts shows, you will want people to know where and when they can see your wares. Make sure that any publicity is timed to coincide with a show opening. If you've established a retail store in an outbuilding on your property with an herb garden out back, your publicity will have a different slant, but days and hours of operation must always be included.

When sending in any news release, expect the media to edit, shorten, and generally mangle the information, as well as rewrite your superb headline. If you are gracious about errors, you will save yourself lots of aggravation and increase the opportunity to have your news releases printed the next time.

A news release should include the elements of any news story: who, what, where, when, why, and how.

Who: Katy Kern.

What: Mother's Day Mad Hatter's Tea Party.

Where: Katy's Herb House, 1901 Main St., Grand Hollow.

When: Saturday, May 1, 1 to 4 P.M.

Why: Enjoy herbal teas and delicacies in the lovely Victorian surroundings of Katy's Herb House. Katy Kern and her staff will be honoring mothers, pouring tea from 1 to 4 P.M. in Victorian gowns and hats with trimmings from the herb garden. Anyone visiting the shop during the tea party in a trimmed hat will receive a gift bag of floral potpourri. Three winners for best hat will receive $10 gift certificates. Katy's Herb House will be filled with a bountiful assortment of handcrafted Mother's Day gifts from the garden.

How: For more information, call 555-1234.

That's a good press release but it would be better if it had a hook—a first line that grabs the reader and entices her to read further. Each story needs one. Here the hook should be the hat party, but that part of the story is buried in the center. Try this instead:

Rummage through the attic for your ancient straw hat. Glorify it with old roses and herbs from the garden. Head down to Katy's Herb House on Saturday, May 1, 1 to 4 P.M., where three winners in the best hat contest will receive . . .

Include the date of release (in this example about ten days before the event) and the name and phone number of the contact person so that the news editor can get additional information. Submit the press release several days before the release date and suggest that the paper send a photographer to cover the event and take a picture of the prizewinning hat.

WORD OF MOUTH

When satisfied customers start advertising for you, you enter nirvana. Unsolicited recommendations are extremely powerful and influence others to come to your door. It is heavenly to know that customers are spreading the word that your creations are outstanding, that you are a true original, that they can get their questions answered and receive the best of service when they purchase something from you—and all this coming from good-will ambassadors for your business.

MARKET RESEARCH

You don't need a lab coat and test tubes for this kind of research; just do what comes naturally to you anyway: ask questions.

The Survey

For our very first open house weekend and our first paid advertising, I selected four papers and ran small display ads. One was the county daily, one a small town daily, one a neighborhood weekly, and the last a weekly advertising tabloid. As each visitor left the barn that weekend, someone was assigned to ask whether the person would like to have her name on our mailing list and how she heard about us. Noted also were the number of buyers who came as a result of a friend who saw an ad. We kept track of who had a Meadow Lark package under her arm. Thankfully, most did. I found what I least expected—that the tabloid was far more productive than the county newspaper. I checked this unexpected result a year later, and the same thing held true.

You must do your own research in order to find out the best opportunities for your business. Every geographical area and every medium is idiosyncratic, and you must judge for yourself. My small advertising budget is obviously weighted most heavily to those places that produce the best results. I continue to advertise in the daily for many reasons, not the least of which is that they list my classes and workshops in their weekly calender of events for free and have published extensive articles with photos about me and my farm. They also have been very cooperative with news releases. Overall, they are a valuable tool in my total marketing program. From the weekly advertiser, I get a good draw from my ads, but no extras. Since they publish no news releases or photos and very few, mostly canned articles, there is no value added to the advertisement.

Compare the number of people who buy as the result of an ad with the cost of the ad including your labor to produce it. My newsletter takes about six hours to design and lay out, and another chunk of time to print out the address labels and stick them on thirty-five hundred mailers. All this must be factored in with the other direct costs, such as printing and postage, and the sales results.

My newsletter cost is high, 22.6 cents to mail bulk rate, 12 cents to print, plus labor, but the return is the highest rate for any advertising I do. After nine years in business, when I do a survey of how people heard about an open house, approximately 75 percent say, "I'm on your mailing list," indicating they're repeat customers, or say a friend who is on the mailing list told them about the event. I also use my newsletter as a brochure that I distribute at talks and demonstrations. There is a savings on postage and labor, so the cost per unit goes down by more than half. And a postcard mailed first-class for 20 cents becomes something of a bargain.

The Coupon
A time-honored way to research effectiveness is to include a coupon in your ad for a product special. You can run the same ad in several print media, but use a different code letter or symbol in each so that you will know the source. That assumes of course that most customers will clip the coupon, and the coupon bargain is for something most people will actually want. An ad rep tried to talk me out of placing a coded ad in her paper and listed all the reasons why people dislike coupons. I think she was afraid her paper couldn't stand up to the test.

THE CONTENT OF YOUR ADS
The KISS principle applies here: Keep It Simple, Stupid. Include your name, location, phone number, hours, simple copy with one or

two clear messages, and your logo. Be sure the type is legible, and include lots of white space.

Your logo must be professionally designed, by you if you have the skills or by someone you pay. It's worth the relatively small initial cost because you will use it for years to come on all your printed materials, including media advertising, newsletters, fliers, cards, letterheads, envelopes, labels, signs, and, when your business grows, bags and gift boxes. I have my logo and business name on my Jeep Cherokee, which I drive constantly, and it is a pleasure to see that the design Don Holohan put together for me eight years ago, a simple and natural stalk of foxtail grass and my name, still represents my business. When I felt the need to change the business name to make it more descriptive and my own name to match my pen name, I was able to use the same logo and simply had the printer insert words where necessary. A good logo will become instantly recognizable and will attract people to your print ads as they scan the page.

For illustrations, use clip art from one of the many series at your local bookstore (ask for the Dover Clip Art series and be sure to check copyright information for your particular use) or computer art provided by your newspaper ad department from their clip art services. You make the selection.

If you are adept in computer graphics, check one of the graphic design software catalogs like *Graphic Express* for a wealth of possibilities. You can often find a student or young illustrator who will draw a simple illustration for you at low cost. If you buy illustrations, make sure you are buying the design outright and can use it again whenever you want. Never buy art for which you will have to pay a reuse fee.

Most ad reps at newspapers can help you set up an ad or do it for you. Most are knowledgeable and the service is free, so use it. Always check the ad before it goes to print.

Time the ad to appear a few days before your event or special promotion. Thursday is a good night for a weekend event. Since the effects of advertising are cumulative, repetition is important. Whenever possible, run the ad a week or more before the event, then repeat it, timing the last insertion to a few days before the event. ∾ **Ask about reduced rates for placing the same ad more than once.**

For your newsletter or fliers that will be inserted in customers' bags, the KISS principle applies. Anytime you design the page layouts and have your flier camera-ready, you cut costs. Whether by going directly to a copy center or to a printer, having prepared fliers duplicated is inexpensive. If you have a computer, you can print your own fliers.

Once you enter computer heaven, you can be lured off the straight and narrow path by the seductiveness of too many choices. I sit before my reliable old Mac and can choose from among sixteen typefaces (fonts), thirty-two font sizes, italics, underlines, boldface, all capitals, outlined letters, and dingbats of infinite shapes. I can change the spacing between letters and lines, condense and enlarge. And I'm only working in black and white! Resist all temptations; use only one or two fonts, no more than three sizes, and only one other menu choice. Choose a font that is clean and legible and you can use on all of your advertising.

The KISS principle applies to radio as well as to print ads: simple copy, a direct message to the individual consumer, repetition, and timing. Research the effects as you would with print ads to help you make decisions on future advertising policy.

QUALITY

Quality should define every aspect of your presentation to the public. With today's computers and spell checkers, there is no excuse for shoddy newsletters, literature, and announcements containing typos and misspellings. There should be no illegible signs or dull-looking announcements on cheap paper. If you can't use a computer and don't want to learn, pay your twelve-year-old to do it for you. She'll do a beautiful job.

Show Off in Photographs

When you need slides or prints for jurying or to accompany press releases, make sure yours are of professional quality, even if you have to pay someone else to take them. Just because you snap treasured pictures of the children and their antics doesn't mean that your knowledge of lighting and styling will pass the finicky standards of the person you are trying to impress.

Show Off in Your Writing

If you feel that your writing skills may not be up to professional standards, get help writing news releases and promotional pieces. Ask someone whose work you admire to edit your pieces. If the budget is tight, offer a custom-made arrangement as payment or trade other skills for writing help, but don't put out shoddy material.

Show Off Your Best Work

Wherever you go, take one grand piece that shows off your finest design skills and your most creative use of materials. The price you have to charge may scare away most potential buyers. The purpose is not to sell, but to demonstrate who you are and what you can do given unlimited resources. It serves as a powerful promotional piece.

Making a Profit

Motivated women and men who expand their hobbies and start to sell their craft wares still delight in giving gifts to friends and family members. They feel guilty about taking money because they enjoy crafting the item. "If it's fun," they think, "I can't charge for it." When selling they price the item solely to recover the cost of the materials, sometimes not even that. Of course, at bargain prices, the crafter becomes overwhelmed with orders and soon decides the pressure is not worth it.

I'm sometimes guilty of the same way of thinking. I spent glorious days in New York and Philadelphia art museums searching for depictions of wreaths to use in the chapter on the history of wreaths in *The Ultimate Wreath Book* (Rodale Press, 1995) and somewhat sheepishly presented my expense receipts to my accountant, who told me he has never found any regulation in the IRS code that prohibits you from enjoying your job.

The difference between a hobby and a business is making a profit. With a hobby you are free to sell items if and when you choose, and perhaps you will cover some of the expenses. In a business, however, you must pay *all* of your expenses, including your salary, *and* return a profit—or there is no point in staying in business. If you can't make a profit, invest in an insured money market fund that guarantees a return.

FINANCING

From the time you start the business, expenses are immediate and never-ending. Whether your business is wholesale or retail, from a shop, a factory, or home, you need enough materials to create a varied and interesting inventory and enough money for publicity, even if it's just business cards and stationery; for travel to shows and show entry expenses; and for the myriad other details involved.

Sit down with the list and categorize the expenses you expect for your first year in business, given your particular niche. Many of the expenses will apply even if you don't have a store. If you hope to participate in six retail shows the first year, list the following:

- Booth rental at each show
- Extra fees for electricity
- Parking at the shows
- Paid labor
- Food, lodging, gasoline, and tolls
- Incidentals away from home
- Required insurance
- Booth construction
- Craft materials and supplies
- Van or truck rental, if necessary

These items represent direct costs and out-of-pocket expenses for doing each show. Your other costs are those that are necessary to run the other aspects of your business at home base. Add up how much money you will need to operate for one year. Get as much factual information as you can, estimate other costs, then add 10 to 20 percent to cover all those myriad details you forgot or underestimated, plus unexpected cost increases, such as jumps in the price of printing because of a paper shortage.

Most people who start a crafts business start small and reinvest in their business as they earn more income. With every sale and every expenditure there is a cash flow. Like a stream, at first it seems that the cash is all flowing away from you, all going out and little coming in. You must have enough cash on hand to pay your bills until your income can cover your expenses and you start to show a profit. For some people it is six months, for others five years, and many get discouraged and get out of business before the red ink ever turns to black. One of the major causes of business failure is not having enough capital at the start to cover the cash flow.

Start small, hold down expenses, continue your day job, work weekends at your craft, save up a small nest egg to get started, borrow from your savings, and get family support. All these are the time-honored ways of crafters in all fields.

The Small Business Administration suggests discussing loans with your bank even before you start in business and setting up your business account where your local banker will be receptive to growing with you. The SBA strongly encourages planning a year in advance and discussing with your banker which month you may need a short-term loan. In your case it may be to cover the expenses of an important crafts show that occurs in November. If you anticipate when you will need some money and when you can pay it back, it is much easier to get the loan. The banker perceives you as being in control of your situation. It is not an emergency, just a normal fluctuation in your business year. When you repay the loan on time, your credit rating will allow you to borrow easily on a short-term basis the next time you need it.

You can borrow money with no interest for at least thirty days if you pay for some items by credit card and then pay in full when the bill comes due. For many people credit cards are fraught with danger, and the interest mounts as you pay other expenses first. It is far better and cheaper to have enough money to invest in yourself before you start in business. Without long-term loans, even if you can get them, you avoid payment of interest year in and year out, which decreases your profits.

REDUCING INVENTORY

Ideally you sell all of your merchandise within two weeks of construction. You pay your bills, order and make more wares, and take your profit. The faster you can turn over your wares, the more profit you can make. Life, of course, is never ideal, and you are always left with slow-moving items and things that you overproduced. You must find a way of getting rid of these items so that your cash flow continues and you have more money to buy and make other things. In addition, your best customers are repeat customers and they always want to see new things even if they always buy the tried and true items.

A time-tested way of moving inventory is by sales and specials. Whether you advertise a grand sale, have specials on certain items, or have a continuous sale table, reducing the price will get rid of lots of stuff you're tired of seeing.

It was my first year at a huge flower show. On the last day of the show, I saw sale signs at many of the vendors' booths. I could understand the fresh flower people because they had nowhere else to market vast quantities of perishables, but I couldn't understand why the basket people were reducing their prices by one-third. As I watched, I saw. The show was a venerable one; people had been coming for years. A tradition had grown up that the last day was sale day, and local people returned to the show just to grab up the bargains. Those who didn't advertise bargains, such as myself, were bypassed even though we had been selling extremely well all week. It didn't take me long to join in the tradition. Quickly calculating in my mind, I found I was still making a profit on the items I chose to reduce, albeit a lesser profit, and was thankful that I had less to pack up to take home and unpack at the other end. My cash flow improved and I was able to move on. At other shows, the tradition among vendors is to reduce nothing on the last day. Check on the custom at each show before you make your decision.

Beware of the woman who flashes three $10 bills, waves them at you, and says that this is all she has for a wreath you've already marked down from $55 to $45 on the last day of the show. She looks so pathetic and deserving, but a quick mental calculation shows you that at $30 you're barely covering your direct expenses. You reject the offer and watch her as she waves more $10 bills up and down the sales floor looking for any takers and buys as many bargains as she can negotiate.

If you sell wholesale, there are large retailers who buy only closeouts to sell at huge discounts. They usually want to buy from you at half of wholesale; they will be doubling the price and can advertise the price truthfully at 50 percent off on all goods. If you are doing a wholesale show, watch for people who come along and ask to buy all of your samples and offer to truck them right out. If this is new merchandise, not your overruns, you might not be interested (unless you hate to pack or don't want the expense of shipping), but get a card for the future. You may be grateful to have it back in your shop when you have lots to clear out.

THE BUSINESS PLAN

All of the academic books on business state that a written plan should be a requirement before getting started. In practice, few craftspeople have a written plan unless they step into a bank. Before lending you money, your banker will want to see your business plan, neatly typed and presented. While you think you can keep in your mind what your own goals are and work toward them, for many people having a written agenda is extremely helpful and may lead to improved performance. The plan commits you to specific achievements in the future.

It is not my intention to write a monograph on how to write a business plan. Your library has many such helps. Know that you will have to have personal data about yourself, your qualifications and experience, and those of your partners, if any. You should present a brief overall summary of the business, your products and services, your marketing plan, including facts about your competition, and all of your financial information, including income, expenses, and cash flow. Your bank may want information going back several years; of course, if you are just starting out, you will only have your projections.

Setting Your Goals
Goals should be realistic and achievable within a stated period of time, and they should be important to you and your business. They should be measurable; otherwise, you will never know if you have accomplished them.

Weak: I'll do some good shows this year. How many is some? What kinds of shows? What does "good" mean?

Strong: I'll sell my wares at three flower shows and three crafts shows this year, including one with an attendance of over fifty thousand.

Weak: I'll work on my public relations plan and get articles in three papers. That's too vague. What do you mean by work? You can't really control whether your articles get published. No matter how good they are and how hard you try, publication is not under your control; therefore, this goal is not well stated.

Strong: I'll send out at least one news release a month to a list of ten media channels. Each release will suggest further ideas for feature articles. I or someone else will write and submit one feature article about my business.

Weak: I need a new look this year in my design. What will you do to achieve it? How will you implement the look?

Strong: I'll design one completely new item each month, construct it in at least five different sizes or versions, and offer it for sale in a test display.

GETTING CREDIT

Credit from your suppliers involves a short-term loan at no interest. If a supplier thinks you are creditworthy, he will sell you merchandise on a promise to pay, usually in thirty days. With good timing on your part, you reduce the number of days from the time you receive the shipment till the time you sell the merchandise, improving your cash flow. An ideal situation for me is one in which a big show occurs on March 1 and I arrange to get a shipment of books on February 15. I can sell the books at the show and, with the income, pay my book bill, keeping the rest for other expenses and profit, of course. With flower supplies, on the other hand, I need more time to design and craft them. Estimate the best delivery date (as distinguished from shipping date) to take into account your cash flow and manufacturing needs.

When you shop at a new supplier, take along a credit sheet, listing your name, address, phone number, business name, bank name, and account number; how many years you've been in business; and three credit references from other companies you buy from. Naturally, the last requirement is the hardest when you start out and seems to be almost impossible, but eventually you will find someone to be the first. Your local flower wholesaler may be willing to risk a small amount of credit, such as $150 to $200. Pay your bills promptly and you're on your way to a golden credit rating.

The advantages of starting small and part-time are that your risks are few; you learn as you grow while the financial pressures are small. Paul Hawken, famous entrepreneur of Smith and Hawken garden catalog and retail stores, in his tape *Growing a Business* recommends that you learn all you can about your business and practice solving problems as they come up. He states that more businesses fail because of lack of imagination than lack of money. You need money to get started and to see if there is a market for your ideas and your craft, but the actual amount can be minimal if you have imagination.

GOOD BUYS

Someone once said that you make a profit by both buying well and selling well. Most of us automatically think of the second half of the formula—pricing, selling, and moving the wares. Fewer people think of the value of buying well.

Ruth Irons, president and chief executive officer of Floral Print, a wholesale manufacturer of a lace and flower giftwear line, says that her primary talent is in sourcing, finding exactly the right lace or ribbon to enhance her elegant designs and knowing her suppliers can deliver. She is constantly scouring the markets for good buys and ones that stimulate her imagination. If she sees a crate of antiqued buttons selling at 90 percent off wholesale, she buys the lot and creates a design to incorporate them.

In a retail business it is even easier to buy well because you can display the bargains you acquire in an attractive setting; when they're gone, they're gone. You don't need to be concerned about back orders and replacing the same items. Sell out one design or line and replace it with a totally different one. As a retailer you have no investment in glossy catalogs, color sheets, or samples sent out to reps and showrooms around the country.

At Wholesale Trade Shows

Look for signs proclaiming "show special." To bolster sales at trade shows, vendors frequently offer special deals. Sometimes it's a 5 to 10 percent discount on all wares in the booth; sometimes it's a rebate on shipping if you order a stated quantity; more often it's a large discount on particular items. If a booth attracts your eye and you don't see a sign, ❧ **ask about show specials.** Sometimes the only designation is a dot sticker on the underside of the price tag.

During my last foray at the New York International Gift Show, I was able to buy some attractive baskets from one of my favorite vendors at 30 percent off wholesale. Beautifully lacquered items were pristine white or forest green, both highly versatile for dried flower and herb designs: white for spring, Mother's Day, or Victorian designs for summer porches, and green for spring or, with burgundy, for Christmas. I asked if these were discontinued items, and I was told no, just an overstock. Regardless, they were perfect for me and I purchased a good quantity of the classic designs.

At Retail Discount Stores

In general I advise you to shun buying at retail for your business, but if you frequent large crafts stores, are familiar with the prices in the wholesale market, and can make quick mental comparisons, you will find temptations. Supplies at discount stores sometimes hover around the price of wholesale; with a sale off the discount price, you may be sitting pretty. This winter I saw picture frames on special at a major crafts discount superstore. They had been reduced twice, and handsome 8-by-10-inch frames were selling for under $5. I resisted only because I wasn't planning to work on pressed-flower pictures again for at least six months. In such situations ask yourself whether you can afford to store unused stock, even a bargain, until you use it.

At Your Flower Wholesaler

If you have a credit account at flower wholesalers, they will mail you advertisements of manufacturers' specials and their own store sales. The three wholesalers that I do business with each have several storewide promotions on supplies, usually 15 percent off everything with no phone orders and no delivery. It's a time to stock up on floral foam, sheet moss, Christmas ribbon, glue sticks, and other staples of your workshop. Don't buy more than you need; there will be another sale in six months.

Develop a relationship with a fresh flower salesperson and call frequently to see what is overstocked or on special from the grower. Make sure she understands that you can't dry *old* flowers and maintain the quality that you need. And make sure *you* can tell the difference by examining the stems, foliage, and flowers. Prices of fresh flowers fluctuate daily and can sometimes be negotiated.

At Flea Markets

Some crafters swear by flea markets and yard sales as the ideal source for unusual containers, picture frames, ribbon, old lace, and other great materials. There's no doubt that bargains abound, but when you factor in the cost of your time to travel, search, and scour, admit that you're doing it as much for the thrill of the hunt as for any true savings. Factor in your travel and shopping time for these supplies.

Additional Savings on Merchandise

There are always savings when you buy case lots of one item. ❧ **Ask vendors about price breaks on items.** One decorative watering can may cost $10 wholesale, ten watering cans $9.50 each, but they are only $9.05 each if you buy twenty-five. Save $23.75 plus some shipping costs by buying the twenty-five if you know you have the market; otherwise, it's no bargain. Buy containers nested in sets, rather than singles. This saves on off-shore shipping to the importer and to you.

Although there are obvious savings of at least 50 percent when buying wholesale, on occasion buying retail still makes more sense. Most, but not all, wholesalers have minimum dollar quantities you must buy. If you're experimenting with a new design and want to try chiffon ribbon to see if it's showy enough, splurge on two yards at the high-end shop in town. If it works, place your $200 minimum order with the manufacturer; if not, you've saved a big bill for a useless item.

Although I buy many of my seed varieties in wholesale quantities at savings, one of the biggest bargains in the world is a retail packet of fifty to one hundred seeds. One packet of lion's ear seeds at $2.45 will produce about fifty plants, more than enough to fill my seasonal needs and wow the visitors to my garden. If one packet can produce sixty plants of yellow strawflowers, do you really want more than that even if you can save money on quantity orders?

REDUCING COSTS

Your method of payment can add up to substantial savings. Avoid finance charges as much as possible. If you have credit, most companies will ship net thirty, with a 1¹/2 percent monthly finance charge if you don't pay within thirty days. Time shipping dates to just before you need the merchandise to help your cash flow. This is always a risk because some manufacturers don't deliver when promised; you will soon learn those that do. When possible get a 2 percent discount by paying within ten days.

Make charges on your credit card, provided you pay them off before any interest accrues. My favorite story involves a proprietor who asks for shipping dates the day after his credit card billing cycle ends. The manufacturer ships and bills the credit card company immediately. The credit card company bills the proprietor after thirty days and gives him another thirty days to pay with no interest. The clever proprietor also accumulates frequent flier miles on his credit card account and enjoys his free trips.

Shipping Costs
Ordinarily you pay the costs of goods coming into your business. Sometimes a vendor will have a special and offer to pay shipping charges with an order at a show or with orders over a set amount. Such an offer can represent a savings of 5 to 10 percent depending on the items and should be examined seriously. Most goods will be shipped UPS, whose rates are computed on a combination of weight and distance. If you have a choice of buying from two vendors who are selling similar products at comparable prices, the one closer to home will save money on shipping costs.

Avoid COD charges—$4.50 at this writing. Some companies charge $4.50 a carton if you are getting multiple cartons, because unscrupulous merchants may receive two cartons one day without a bill and the third carton, which has the charge attached, the next day. By refusing the third carton, the merchant has two cartons of goods for which he has paid no shipping charges, and the angry, frustrated manufacturer has trouble recovering the loss.

I once got a shipment of six cartons of containers, each with a $4.50 COD charge—$22.50 above what I should have paid—

added to the regular shipping costs. In this case, I was the irate and frustrated party. I called the manufacturer to complain and received a credit.

Some manufacturers now forgo COD completely because more buyers are refusing COD orders at the shop doorstep. The manufacturer then must absorb the packing and shipping costs as well as the COD charge, not a happy situation.

Check delivery costs from your local flower wholesaler and compare them with the value of picking up the supplies yourself. Delivery charges keep going up, but there are usually savings on delivery as you order more goods. When possible, pile up your order until you absolutely need it, instead of ordering a small amount every week. You may feel that some of these suggestions are nickel-and-diming, but it's important from the start to think of keeping costs low. Your employees will pick up this attitude from you and will absorb the business ethic of saving where possible.

BREAKAGE AND DETERIORATION

Breakage and deterioration contribute to the high cost of flowers and herbs. With fresh materials, deterioration is a natural part of the aging process. Even before cut flowers die, their petals may be bruised or their stems left out of water too long.

Early in my career I sold fresh-cut, field-grown flowers to several local florists. One of these was owned by a vibrant, friendly woman who had built up her busy shop to be the favorite in the area. Her worktables were always cluttered with containers, old silks, and trailing ribbons. The designers had to claim a square foot of table space each time they needed to create an arrangement. I sold the shop a box of fresh-cut tulips one day and was surprised when the proprietor called two days later with a large reorder. She confessed that my first box had gotten lost in the shuffle and hadn't made it into the cooler. She indicated that this was not an infrequent occurrence. I continued to wend my way through the cartons every time I delivered an order; the shop was organized only after it was sold. Dead flowers are fit only for the compost heap—a total loss not only of the goods but also of the time to pay the bill and reorder merchandise.

If you are using dried rather than fresh flowers, timing is just as critical. Flowers and herbs left too long in the field will mature past their prime and will frequently drop their petals or lose their color when dried. You increase costs by having to discard materials that could have been of excellent quality if picked in time.

All the cost of growing the plants comes to nothing if they are killed by an early frost. I left for a late-September flower show admiring a three hundred-foot row of brilliantly colored celosia in my field, expecting to harvest the week I returned. I discovered the hard way that cockscomb blackens if the temperature drops even one degree below freezing. The plants continued to grow, mocking my imprudence with an ebony crust on top of every comb. It was a total loss and cost an additional $500 when I had to buy what I needed from another grower that year.

Dried materials shipped in will have some flower heads rolling around the bottom of the carton. Some breakage is inevitable. Also inevitable is breakage when you are constructing your arrangements. Here the glue gun is frequently the savior; many a blossom gets reattached with no one the wiser. We also keep trays of "brokies," material with some or all of the stems broken off, separated by type of flower or foliage or by color. Our "brokies" find themselves glued onto hats, wreaths, swags, and the like; made into our wrapped minibouquets, which are inexpensive pickup items often purchased by or for children; used in our potpourris; or packaged into "Meadow Lark Craft Packs," a selection of loose flower heads we sell to others making their own crafts. Think of other ways of transforming broken stems into lovely, salable merchandise.

Dried flowers and herbs deteriorate over time; this natural deterioration is hastened by humidity and sunlight. Colors change and fade. Humidity causes some botanicals to droop. An exceptionally dry atmosphere makes the materials overly brittle. Insects may attack. Even eucalyptus loses its smell over time. Learn to compare and recognize the difference in color and appearance of the highest-quality materials, the freshest, best dried, most carefully stored, and start your designs only with materials in their prime.

One way to determine quality is to check the stem color of dried materials. German statice is a good example. It is an easy-to-grow perennial in horticultural Zones 4 to 8. Cut when mature and hung in a warm, dark dry spot, the stems stay green and the flowers (bracts) stay bright white for over a year. When German statice is old or poorly dried, the flower heads are white with a beige cast, and the stems are brownish. This deterioration has an unfortunate effect on the overall product that becomes apparent when one sees two German statice wreaths side by side.

If you don't grow your own statice, you may prefer to purchase some very fresh from a floral wholesaler and dry it yourself. No flower dries more easily, but some wholesalers treat statice with disdain. Knowing how easy it is to dry, they leave it in the carton in which it was shipped from California, rather than giving it precious space in the walk-in cooler. By the time you get it, it may have been in the carton for a week, not dried, but no longer fresh, and the stems may have already started to turn brown. Call the wholesaler and ask for the date when it will come in. Buy and hang it to dry immediately. If that doesn't work, avoid the shoddy stuff and go instead for that already dried by a quality grower. ✐ **Ask for samples to be sent if buying by mail order.** Expect to be billed for them, but it's worth it to see what you'll be getting. ✐ **Ask for this year's crop and tell the grower you will return anything old.** Learn to "reconstitute" statice as well as some other dried materials by misting with water and leaving them to relax in a large black plastic garbage bag, tied tightly for about two hours. The crush from shipping will disappear.

Each flower and herb has its preferred timing for picking and preferred method of drying. For example, if you're growing globe thistle (*Echinops*), learn to harvest it when the blue color is most intense, just before the petals burst forth. School yourself on each species by talking to other growers, observing carefully, and reading books like *Flower Crafts: A Step-by-Step Guide to Growing, Drying & Decorating with Flowers*, by Ellen Spector Platt.

Oversupply

It sounds like a happy problem. The rain was plentiful; the sun was brilliant; and you had bumper crops of many flowers. You harvested twice as much larkspur as you normally sell. You hate to just pitch leftovers to make way for the new crop. Think creatively. Add a class in larkspur wreaths to your fall list; give one bunch of free larkspur with each purchase of ten or more bunches of any flower. Use more larkspur in your arrangements this year than you normally do. Plan a display around the Nancy Drew *Mystery of Larkspur Lane*. Design a Christmas tree draped with garlands of larkspur. Don't let it just sit there!

Donations

As I prepare to compost last year's leftovers, I set aside still-acceptable materials with some remaining color and donate some boxes to a horticultural therapy program at a psychiatric hospital, whose patients make items for resale. Another large carton goes to the Pennsylvania Horticultural Society, whose fall Harvest Show includes a children's activity tent. There, kids construct their own small arrangements. (Many times mothers can't keep their hands away and clandestinely complete their own.) These charitable donations of usable materials should be recorded and may be claimed as tax deductions if current regulations permit.

Inefficient Labor Practices

There are those who can't work and talk at the same time. When their mouths open, their hands stop working. Pulling weeds by hand is not the most interesting activity, and for me, talking makes the time fly faster. Train workers from the start that talk must be done while heads are down and work is performed. It's easier when you are working alongside your trainee and can show her how fast you can weed a row and still describe the movie you saw last weekend or talk about your upcoming crafts show. Weeding time is a good planning time, as hands are busy, but minds usually are not.

Watch two people bunch flowers newly harvested from the fields. One picks up a handful, discards rejected flowers back in the cart, and wraps the bunch with a rubber band. The next handful of flowers plucked from the cart contains the discards from the first bunch, plus new discards. These all go back into the cart. The woman I saw do this had an advanced college degree. What could she have been thinking? The second worker places all discards in a separate pile to compost at the end of the day. Don't assume that because the task is very simple, it will be done efficiently. You must look at your own efficiency as well as that of anyone you employ and gently shape behavior to what you need.

Decide on the standard you want and can afford. Your goal is quality, but affordability must also be factored in. If I want to keep my bunches affordable, I may have to forgo having all flower heads perfectly aligned and having the stems cut evenly at the bottom after they are packed with a rubber band. The quality of the flowers themselves is as high as I can make it, but I skimp on the packaging of the bunch to reduce labor costs and keep the price down. Perhaps some day I'll invest in a stem cutter (it's like a giant paper cutter) and neaten up the bottoms of the bunches. Till then, they have the "natural" look.

We rarely use an assembly line since each product is one of a kind, but if we're making thirty-five centerpieces, all containers are prepared with foam and moss ahead of time and all bows are made in advance. Then the treat of inserting the flowers is completed individually. Similarly, when I make pressed-flower note cards, I assemble all of the materials, spread out the pressed flowers on waxed paper where they are accessible, and get out glue, tweezers, and other tools. I design in sets of ten each, with one color background and one combination of flowers. After making ten cards, I go on to another ten with a different color background, a different combination of flowers, and a different design. In this way I can combine efficiency with individuality. I usually work with one other employee, who gets training as we work and ask can questions about her design.

Losses from Light Fingers

To me "shrinkage" is what happens to flowers during the drying process. But in the retail trade it's a theft, whether by an employee or a customer. We all like to think that our employees are honest and loyal, and I know that mine are, but as I read many books about business, theft keeps turning up as an important loss factor. You will develop your own methods of reducing loss from thievery. When you are heavily involved in all aspects of a small business, you have a good method of keeping track of losses. You know how busy you are on a particular day, and you know what is selling. The better the relationship you have with your employees, the less likely they are to cheat.

Theft from customers is reported to be an ever-increasing problem, but I am not about to put up mirrors and cameras in my barn. I have found more of a problem at large flower shows where one or two items disappear overnight, usually the biggest or most expensive. I often picture my most beautiful dried topiary, which disappeared overnight, adorning the table of the security guard's mother. Reduce thievery by fashioning overnight covers for your display. Many flower vendors wrap their whole booths in drop cloths to deter walk-by grabbing of merchandise.

COLLECTIONS

Will you accept cash only? What will you do about checks, credit cards, and charge accounts? There are pros and cons to each, and I will list some of these so that you can form your own judgment.

Cash Only

The advantage is that you get paid on the spot.

The disadvantage is that fewer and fewer people are carrying large amounts of cash in their wallets. If they don't have the cash they can't make spontaneous, unexpected purchases, thus limiting your sales opportunities. Since craft items are always nonessentials, you need a way to make a purchase easier.

Checks
The advantage of checks is that you get paid on the spot. People tend to purchase more expensive items than they have cash for.

The disadvantage is that you run the risk of accepting a bad check. Some vendors take driver's license ID to try to prevent problems. I stopped requiring ID after several years at big flower shows where I received no bounced checks. Customers are surprised that I don't ask for ID and many offer it spontaneously. I make eye contact and reply that I've never had a bad check in all my years in business, and I don't think theirs would be the first. They laugh with embarrassed pleasure. If I did have a bad check, short of calling the person and asking for a new check, I think the time and effort involved to prosecute would be far greater than the loss on any sale.

Credit Cards
With credit cards you get paid as soon as you deposit the slips in your bank account. People buy more expensive items than they have cash for. They often buy more spontaneously, as some customers seem to have the impression that a credit card is free money. They are willing to pay interest for their purchases.

The disadvantage of credit cards is that the bank will charge you 3 to 5 percent of each sale to start; the cost goes down the more you use the service. The fee is somewhat negotiable. Another disadvantage is the requirement that you get an authorization for each sale in order to ensure payment. Here again I absorb my own risk as most of my purchases are under $100, and it is extremely inconvenient for me to have each purchase authorized at a busy show. On sale days at those shows, I stow my credit card paraphernalia and accept only cash.

Be aware that if you want to take credit cards for phone orders you need special authorization from the credit card company. Ask your bank to give you the phone number to call for this service.

Charge Accounts

Corporate clients expect charge accounts and usually will pay only once a month. They are valuable if you receive many phone orders for local delivery or shipping. If you sell wholesale, your customers will expect to receive credit, net thirty. Before you extend it, make sure you do credit checks on your customers.

The main disadvantage is that your money is tied up for at least thirty days, and probably more. If you bill every thirty days, and offer terms of net thirty, potentially it will be sixty days until you see a return. Make sure your statements include the terms of payment and monthly interest charges for overdue bills. This will avoid some problems but not all. The larger the account, the more the company seems to think it can ignore payment terms.

My worst account was a local hospital that placed a big order for flowers for a special celebration. They paid their large (for me) bill after four months and after much prodding on my part. I later found out their cash flow problems were monumental; for several years they paid only the vendor who screamed the loudest, once stopped paying for the health insurance of their employees, and just recently failed to meet their payroll. As a small business you are at the mercy of large accounts. Although experiences like this are not frequent, they happen, and come as a shock to one's innocence.

In a wholesale business where the invoices will run in the hundreds of dollars, credit checks of new accounts are necessary. Check credit references and with one of the large credit bureaus or be prepared to be burned. Offer to ship COD, on a valid credit card, or pro forma to minimize problems. (With pro forma accounts, call the customers when the merchandise is ready to ship, and ship upon payment of a valid check. Most companies wait for the check to clear before shipping.)

PROTECT YOUR INVENTORY

Part of the mystique of dried flowers is in capturing and preserving the fresh look of the garden. There are several strategies that will help you maintain quality:

1. Don't buy more dried materials than you will need for a three- or four-month period. Try to estimate accurately when you will need to reorder. The distributor's storage facilities are likely to be climate-controlled and better than most small businesses can afford.

2. Store excess materials carefully with insect repellents, such as moth balls or Indian moth pheromone traps, in lidded cardboard boxes.

3. Pack the boxes loosely. Cramming will ruin the shape of dried materials and make every bunch a pancake.

4. Sell as soon as possible after construction. I am in a perpetual conflict between making a generous supply of finished arrangements so that the barn looks bountiful and keeping the displayed inventory modest enough to protect my valuable flower stock from exposure to the inevitable light and humidity problems of the Pennsylvania climate.

5. Devise a system to date edible, culinary, and medicinal herbs, whether they were shipped to you or harvested from your own field. These herbs lose their flavor and potency when old, so careful storage in cool, airtight conditions will help longevity. ✒

Deposits on Custom Orders

Deposits are a necessary part of doing business for all individual and some company accounts. You secure one-quarter to one-third of the final cost, specified in writing as nonrefundable before you start the job. This deposit minimizes last-minute cancellations. In the bridal business many charges are prepaid. No bride walks out of the bridal shop with her gown, still owing on it. No food is served at a reception without a deposit to hold the date and full payment before the dinner. No band plays without cash changing hands. Flowers are no different.

I take deposits for all custom work, write the order in as much detail as possible as to size, color, shape, style, even many of the flowers involved, price, and tax. I learned to specify the time by which the item must be picked up. On the few times the customer has been dissatisfied with the finished product, I worked very hard to correct it to her satisfaction. Only once was I unable to satisfy a customer and insisted she take back her deposit as I felt she was chronically dissatisfied and unable to be pleased.

There are no disadvantages that I can think of. Customers expect to pay a deposit for special work and feel that it is a reasonable charge.

WHAT TO DO WITH ALL THOSE SAVINGS

You've shopped well, taken advantage of discounts, sales, and specials, saved on shipping, and reduced your costs. You can pass along the savings on certain items and declare specials of your own. Or you can sell at the regular retail price and reap a higher profit margin. Your decision will vary from time to time, but the choice is yours. I just visited a lovely gift shop in New York City where they offered Mexican pottery sold in sets by the manufacturer. I noted that the offering price treated each item as a single unit and didn't pass along to the customer the almost 40 percent savings the store received for buying as a set. No doubt the store will use the profit to balance some other items where they bought less well.

CHAPTER TEN

Pricing

Sue, a student in one of my business workshops, had started a business selling wreaths and arrangements of dried, silk, and preserved materials. She took orders at work for custom pieces and started getting commissions for wedding work—for the bridal party, ceremony site, and reception. Sue was hoping to develop that aspect of her business. She had no resale number and paid 6 percent sales tax on everything she bought. Most of her purchases were made at a large discount crafts store about five miles from her home. Each time she got an order she would travel to buy her supplies and found that the extras were piling up in her workshop, as she often didn't use all the materials in one design. She charged her client for the cost of materials used plus her design time, but didn't factor in the time she spent purchasing special materials, discussing the wedding with her client, delivering and installing the arrangements, or helping the bride with last-minute details. She had lots of commissions because her prices were far below the competition, but she was getting fed up with her business, feeling she was working too hard with too little to show for it. Sue had only the vaguest idea of what was wrong, that she was overpaying and undercharging.

HOW TO DECIDE ON A PRICE

Let's start with several important assumptions:

1. You want to pay yourself an hourly wage.

2. You want to make a profit on the investment of time and money for your business venture.

3. You want to price your merchandise fairly so that you don't cheat yourself or your customer.

4. You don't feel that you must have the lowest prices but that you must give value.

In practice, flower and herb designers use different formulas to determine the price. Some just look at the finished piece and mutter that it looks like a $50 wreath. Some know to the penny the cost of every item that went into the wreath. Whenever you want to add a few more flowers here and there to make it look "better," think of the cost of each additional stem, and get comfortable with the idea that a $50 arrangement will not be as luscious as a $75 one, that adding another rose to a $15 bud vase now gives you a $19 bud vase, and you must charge accordingly or lose money.

The Amateur Formula

The amateur formula is based on the following statements:

1. I grew the flowers on my own land and cut them from perennial plants I had, so the flowers are free.

2. The wire and glue stick cost me less than a dollar.

3. My labor is free since I made it in my spare time.

4. If I can sell a small herb wreath for $10, I'm making $9 profit.

This formula is for the hobbyist, not the businessperson. Look what happens when you sell all your small herb wreaths and want to make more. You've run out of flowers and need to buy them; you need to pay someone to help you and your teenage daughter wants, not unreasonably, as much as she would earn at Burger King. You suddenly find you are shelling out all the money on expenses and have nothing for the kitty at the end of the show. Let's try another hobby.

If you are serious about your business, amateurs create a dangerous competitive pricing situation. If a hobbyist has a booth at a crafts show along with other serious crafters who are trying to make a living selling their wares, it is cold comfort that the amateur will be out of the business in six months or will start to price competitively; there will soon be someone else along to take her place. Look before you leap into a show to see what the competition is. When you gently turn down the neighborhood crafts show, you do it partly to protect yourself from hobby-priced competition that can leave your sales plummeting.

Keystoning

In the gift industry it used to be accepted practice to buy an item from the manufacturer and double the price to sell at retail. You took a basket out of the carton, marked it up 100 percent (multiply the wholesale cost by two), and put it on the shelf for sale. Now some stores, especially those in high-rent areas, are starting to multiply by 2.2 to 2.5 to ensure a profit margin. This formula works because the only labor involved is checking against an invoice, pricing, and displaying. Keystoning is one way to establish a price on finished goods that you offer for resale, like containers, oils, and crafts supplies.

List Price

If you buy books for resale, the retail price is usually printed on the cover. You can buy books at 40 to 60 percent off the cover price, depending on the publisher, the quantity you order, and the returnability of the books. Of course, you can sell books at a discount, matching some of the large chains, but no one will buy a book marked above the list price.

A Retail Florist's Pricing

The retail florist uses the following steps to set her prices:

1. List the wholesale cost of all hard goods—container, foam, wire, picks, and ribbon. Double the cost for the retail price of hard goods.

2. List the cost of all perishables—flowers, foliage, and fruit. Mark up three to five times depending on your locale. This is the retail price of the flowers.

3. Add 1 and 2 for the retail price of goods. Multiply by 20 to 35 percent for the cost of labor. The lower figure of 20 percent is for the cost of standard items in your design repertoire; the higher figure is for custom party and wedding work involving consultations and installation. Note that the cost of labor is figured as a percentage of the cost of the goods rather than on an hourly basis.

Jim Morley, editor-in-chief of *Professional Floral Design* magazine, suggests you go one step further. "When you are figuring the selling price after the arrangement is completed," he recommends, "first add up the retail cost of the material. Then divide the retail cost of the material total by the reciprocal of the labor percentage (the reciprocal of the labor percentage is determined by subtracting the labor percentage from 100)." So, for example, if your labor percentage is 20 percent of the cost of the goods, divide by the reciprocal, 80 percent; if your labor percentage is 35 percent, divide by the reciprocal, 65 percent. This calculation gives you the selling price of the arrangement.

Example: pricing a dried arrangement

basket	$ 5.00	
foam	.50	
moss	.35	
ribbon	1.50	
total hard goods		7.35 x 2 = 14.70
10 freeze-dried roses	15.00	
bunch of avena	1.85	
1/2 bunch of gypsophila	3.00	
total flowers		19.85 x 3.5= $69.48
total materials		$84.18
total cost (labor = total materials divided by 80%)		$105.22

The selling price of this lovely basket of freeze-dried roses is $105. If you feel this is too expensive to sell in your shop, rather than just slashing the finished price and making it unprofitable to sell, substitute a bunch of larkspur for half of the roses. Let's see what a difference this would make in the cost.

total hard goods		$14.70
5 freeze-dried roses	$7.50	
bunch of avena	1.85	
1/2 bunch of gypsophila	3.00	
bunch of larkspur	1.85	
total flowers		14.20 x 3.5 = $49.70
total materials		$64.40
total cost (labor = total materials divided by 80%) $80.50		

The selling price of this lovely basket of mixed materials with freeze-dried roses is $79.95. It is just as big as the first arrangement but sells for $25 less because of the substitution of larkspur for five roses. Use air-dried roses and you reduce the price again by about $15.

Wholesale Pricing

Artisans who sell wholesale know from the start that the stores they sell to will probably keystone the wares—that is, double the wholesale price to resell to the customer. There must be enough profit in manufacturing for you and then enough leeway that the customer is still willing to buy the item. If you sell wholesale, you can afford to take a smaller markup than the person who sells retail because there should be an economy of scale. You are buying raw materials in quantity; therefore, you should get a much better price. You are selling and shipping in quantity; therefore, the cost of sales is lower.

A typical method of wholesale pricing is as follows:
1. Direct costs of all the materials involved per item
2. Direct labor costs (time to make the item x hourly wage)
3. Add #1 and #2
4. Multiply by 2.5 to 2.75

If you are manufacturing the basket of freeze-dried roses for the wholesale market, you can reduce the cost of all items by buying in greater quantities and placing advance orders. I estimate that you can save at least 20 to 30 percent over the regular wholesale cost. A shop that is buying in tens can't compete in price negotiations with you who are buying in hundreds or even thousands.

Instead of buying dried flowers through normal wholesale channels, you can get distributor prices, order in container lots, or buy directly from growers. As your needs grow, so should your purchasing ability, keeping costs low enough to absorb all the doubling and percentage increases at each stage of the distribution chain. Don't forget the rep will get 15 percent of your gross sales right off the top.

The Craft Consultant's Formula

For many years our local art center was blessed with a specialist in crafts marketing. Merle Walker, former director of the Schuylkill County Council for the Arts and former executive director of the League of New Hampshire Craftsmen, is now a full-time consultant in the arts. In the sixties and seventies she advised many crafts dreamers, people who were absorbed solely in their production, on how to become more businesslike and profitable in their approach. A weaver herself, and having worked mostly with crafts like pottery, glassblowing, woodworking, and weaving, she says she has seen this approach work just as well in the flower and herb crafts.

It starts with complete record keeping of all income and expenses. You must do this anyway for tax purposes, so use your records to help you in pricing as well. Here are some definitions:

Hourly rate: the amount of money you pay yourself for labor per hour (gross hourly wage before deductions and taxes). This figure must be realistic, neither exaggerated nor minimized. Think of what it would cost you per hour to get a person with similar construction skills to replace you. Here we are not talking about design but construction skills.

The hourly rate is actually different for each task you perform. If you are a workshop of one, doing everything from sweeping the floor to keeping the books to advertising, you know that to replace yourself at each step you would pay a different rate.

Labor: how long it takes you to make an item. Time yourself on making a *set* of items—for example, twelve herb wreaths. Use the time for a set, rather than the time to make one, because there is always a labor savings on making a set. Multiply by your hourly rate. Divide by the number you made to get the average labor cost for one.

Materials: the ingredients for the set of small herb wreaths, including the wire base, clamps, glue sticks, artemisia, lavender, sage, basil, and safflower. Disregard the cost of the glue gun or any other reusable equipment.

The pricing formula looks like this:

labor for one item	$3.00
materials cost for one item	+ 9.00
	$12.00
30% for general and administrative	+ 3.60
	$15.60
20% profit	+ 3.12
wholesale price	$18.72

This is your wholesale price, at which you sell to stores.

To get the retail price, double $18.72 to 37.44 and round to your preferred total, perhaps $37.50. The crafts world is full of people who underprice their retail goods and then, when a catalog or other wholesale opportunity comes along, they can't afford the sale because they can't drop their prices in half and still make any money.

In the example above, if you sell the wreath at a show for $18.75, which is the wholesale price rounded off, and then try to cut the price in half to sell to a shop, you are selling below the price of labor plus materials at $9.38 and are not only failing to make a profit, but are taking money out of your pocket and giving it away with every wreath.

Another way of working this formula is to figure backward from the amount of money you need to earn in a year in order to determine how many productive hours you need in a day. By *productive*, Merle Walker means the time you spend actually producing the craft; exclude the time spent on your business, writing press releases, designing items in your head, comparison shopping, and selling at shows. If you define an income you want to make for the year and a per hour income, follow this formula to determine how many hours you need for production. Let's say the gross salary you desire is $15,000. Divided by 230 workdays, this equals $65 per day. The predetermined salary per hour is $10; therefore, you need to work 6.5 hours per day.

You can easily see that you must work at production for the better part of each day to earn a rather small salary. Then when do you do all the other work tasks? You will need to work more hours or more days. Remember too that you will be earning some profit on each sale. Craftspeople, like antique dealers, are used to working long hours to earn a living wage, and the ultimate per hour salary for all work is often way below the minimum. The compensations are in the craft itself and the ability to live the kind of life you prefer, with its attendant freedom. If you want a higher hourly compensation, you should consider working for Microsoft.

What the Traffic Will Bear

Is there an entrepreneur who hasn't looked at a finished design with a price carefully calculated by the preferred formula and nudged the price upward a bit because it looked like it was worth more? One of your continuous research tasks is to be scouting for comparable prices for your wares. Look at catalogs, shops, and retail and wholesale shows to do a reality check. If your prices are much lower for an item of comparable quality, there must be a reason. Very likely, it's because you are undercharging. If your prices are much higher, there must also be a reason; perhaps your expenses are higher working in an expensive area. Try to establish the facts before you change your prices, and if you can't, seek help from a knowledgeable person, such as your accountant, an SBA consultant, or a marketing specialist.

Further Advice

The Crafts Report has published a booklet entitled *Some Helpful Hints on Pricing Craft Work* with five short articles on pricing for craftspeople. They all involve keeping careful records of time and expenses but slightly different ways of arriving at a final price. Although most of the examples are given for potters, they are easily translatable for any craft business. The main difference is that depreciation of equipment will be less of a factor with flower and herb crafters, as glue guns and clippers can be considered disposable. Your biggest expense may be for a vehicle, and usage will probably be shared between personal and business needs.

Many people with accounting backgrounds who write about pricing ask you to figure overhead, fixed, and variable costs, and determine how many items you will be making to see how the fixed costs drop per item as the number of that item increases.

After I read some of the complicated analyses involved, I think of applying them to my own small retail business. I always stop short. If I make two dozen herbal wall hangings on a birch twig base, I go on to create the next item. Since my business involves many one-of-a-kind items, I need to be able to work out a price quickly. I shudder to think of my profit dissipating into accounting time.

On the other hand, formulas that use a fixed percentage for overhead may be underestimating your actual costs. Said in a less polite way, are you overspending on your fixed costs? Check your actual overhead at the end of each year to see that the actual total fixed costs for the year equal the percentage allocated to your price.

FANTASY PRICING AND DESIGNER LABELS

As with designer clothing, there are also designer flowers, arranged by the floral designer of the moment. The price is not related to the time and materials involved but to the cachet of the designer. In the late eighties I was roaming the Rue Cherche Midi in Paris on holiday and was captivated by the elegance of the dried flowers displayed in the windows of Jules des Pres. It was the first time I had seen the new stacked designs, soon after to become fashionable in this country. My husband, who calls most flowers either gladiolas or lilies, was almost as impressed. But we looked at each other in horror as we calculated prices. Table arrangements were selling at over $2,000 apiece. Fragrant orange pomanders, precisely constructed versions of the kind we used to produce in Girl Scouts, were selling for $30 to $35 each. I learned in chatting with the store manager that the shop numbered movie stars and high political figures among its clientele. If you can count on a similar clientele, you can also command fantasy prices. Most of us can't.

You may choose to make a lower profit margin on an item for a specific reason. For example, for a one-of-a-kind item that you make for its PR value or to stop traffic at a show, you may want to calculate at a special price to sell after the event, especially if it is large and unwieldy and not worth packing and unpacking again at home.

Once I increased the price of an intricate dried fruit Della Robbia wreath because I knew I would need it for a photograph in a month, and I didn't want to make another unless well remunerated. When a customer wanted it badly enough to pay the somewhat elevated price, she and I were both content with the deal.

UPGRADES AND DOWNGRADES

Whether you're working with a bride, decorating a holiday home, or making arrangements for a special event, there are opportunities to suggest and sell more than the customer originally had in mind. Such sales naturally enhance the profitability of the event for your business. Often the customer is grateful when you make a suggestion that will add a note of luxury, such as a special bouquet for the powder room or small flower baskets clustered in tiers on a sideboard for guests to take home.

Never let the flower expenses exceed the customer's budget. However, be very leery of offering a discount, which could cheapen your product value in the eyes of the customer. Instead, suggest ways to reduce the overall costs, such as the following:

1. Omit one or two of the items on the list, while making the remaining items as eye-catching as possible.

2. Use the customer's own container when making a massive arrangement.

3. Suggest unusual flowers that are in season and are plentiful.

WHEN BUSINESS IS TOO GOOD

Before starting this book, as I interviewed craftspeople creating all kinds of designs, both in and out of the flower and herb field, I spoke to people I knew had once made beautiful things and were now out of the business. In each case, I expected tales of how hard the work was and how badly things had turned out. To my amazement, the first three people in my decidedly nonrandom sample said that business had been too good.

Meet Anne. I had seen her first in my barn when she turned up to buy a few bunches of flowers, then in two of my workshops and at a plant swap. Young, energetic, and married with two young children, she had an intense feeling for and knowledge about growing things. Her goal was to start a business of her own. Her designs, incorporating local wildflowers with purchased materials, were charming and original. Over several years I spoke to her from time to time on the phone and knew that she had started on the show circuit. When next I saw her she was out of business. Why? Business got too good. She went to some fall shows; at each she sold out and took orders for more arrangements. As Christmas neared, she became overwhelmed. Although she managed to complete her orders, Anne recognized that she would have to hire help come spring. She told me she didn't want the responsibility of paying wages, making deductions, and handling taxes. She stopped in her tracks and veered off in another direction, while never losing her dream of someday being involved with flower farming.

POSITIONING YOUR PRODUCT

I sell note cards decorated with pressed flowers, collages of decorative papers, and snippets of ribbon. Complete with an envelope and encased in a cellophane bag, each note card costs more than a typical Hallmark card, but sales are brisk. As I listen to customers discuss their purchases with their shopping companions, I realize that most were planning to discard the envelopes and frame the cards for a powder room or as small hostess gifts. These customers have found a true bargain, a $3.95 custom-designed picture that will fit into an inexpensive ready-made frame. As note cards they might be on the expensive side, but as pictures they are a great value. If I position the product differently, can I sell as many without the envelope, saving .28 cents, and increase the cost to 4.50? It's time to do some market research. ✂

Kathryn had been an art teacher before her first child was born and wanted to stay home to care for her baby. Her husband taught drafting and printing. They started a home-based T-shirt business and worked hard to get orders from around the country. Their business was wholesale, which meant designing, printing, packing, shipping, and selling quantities of T-shirts. As their business took off, T-shirts overran their home. Fumes from paint and print became a potential problem. They started looking for space to buy and set up a small plant, but were reluctant to take on the financial risk of either a long term lease or a mortgage and investment in equipment and employees. They sold the business. Kathryn is now looking at another home-based craft business, with a much more compact product.

When you have a home-based craft business, you have the advantage of flexibility in your work schedule, and you reduce out-of-pocket expenses. The disadvantage is that you can never get away from your business. The phone can ring at any time; the flowers can overflow into other rooms of your house. You are tempted to work seven days a week and extremely long hours because you can easily run in and do one more thing. As with any home-based business, whether writing, computer consulting, or crafts, you will probably have to be very firm with friends who call or stop in during your workday, thinking you are dying for an interruption, or not thinking at all. And you will have to deal with your own temptations to run downstairs and throw in a couple loads of wash or start dinner when you still should be in your flower mode.

CHAPTER ELEVEN

The Business of Business

A business is a legal entity. There are three basic business structures to select from. Most craft businesses start as individual proprietorships, where there is a sole owner of the business. Under an *individual proprietorship*, even if you hire people you are solely responsible and reap all the profit and absorb all the loss. Your business expenses and income are declared on Schedule C of your personal (or joint with your spouse) income tax. Profit or loss from your business is factored into your personal tax and the tax rate you pay is based on your total personal income. An individual proprietorship is the simplest of the three business structures.

A *partnership* between two or more people is a legal entity, and you should get help from your attorney in setting it up. The partnership income schedule goes in with your personal taxes.

Partnerships often start out with spouses, and the two may decide that one will keep a day job while the other builds up the craft business; in time both hope to work full-time in the business. Whether the partnership is between friends or spouses, clarifying the roles at the outset reduces the likelihood of pain later. Often one person is the creative member of the team, responsible for design, display, and merchandise; the other is the business manager, responsible for the books, the records, and the bills. Roles and duties of each partner should be detailed. You should know in advance and have a written partnership agreement detailing what happens if one partner moves away, gets sick, or wants out of the business for any reason. Must you buy her out? At what price? How will the payout be made? Is she free to open a similar business near you and compete? Is she free to discuss partnership business with others? Don't get into a partnership unless you know the terms for getting out of it. As with a will, the agreement is useful only if it is updated regularly, as conditions of the business change.

A *corporation* is a separate legal entity with regulations of its own that you must follow. There are substantial governmental and legal fees for setting up a corporation. The corporation pays its own taxes, at a different, usually higher rate than an individual. Many craftspeople change from a proprietorship into a corporation only when the income, liabilities, and number of employees grow substantially.

Don't try to set up your business entirely on your own, unless you have the expertise to do so. Experts abound who can help you on an hourly basis, and availing yourself of their services makes both logical and financial sense if you can prevent expensive problems from cropping up in the future.

THE LEGALITIES

An attorney can advise you of the procedures and benefits to you of an individual proprietorship, a partnership, or a corporation. Your attorney will understand not only the general benefits and drawbacks of the legal structures, but also how they will affect your individual circumstances. My attorney dissuaded me from starting a corporation at the outset, as the extra expense wasn't justified by the small liability involved. If you want help registering the fictitious name of your business, an attorney can be helpful there as well.

ACCOUNTING

As you are starting your business, it is very helpful to discuss your accounting system with a professional. She can set up a record-keeping system for you and help you decide whether your accounting system will be on a cash basis or on an accrual basis. If your business is on a cash basis, you declare income when it is received and expenses when they are paid. On an accrual basis, you declare income when it is billed and expenses when they are incurred. The accountant will explain inventory requirements and depreciation regulations.

When you grow large enough to have employees, the accountant can help you with the forms and procedures needed for deductions and payroll. She can tell you the latest regulations on home business deductions, such as deducting your home office, workshop, or shop on your personal taxes, and if so, how much you can deduct. Yes, you can do all of this yourself if you are knowledgeable in the tax laws and regulations, which change with some frequency. You can read the appropriate materials and go from agency to agency to get the appropriate forms or wait on hold while the canned music plays for fifteen minutes until you reach the appropriate person who will send you the forms. I started to collect all the materials for payroll deductions myself and got fed up after two hours with little results. Deciding I was being penny-wise and pound-foolish, I hied to my accountant's office, where the office manager gave me every federal, state, and local form I needed in ten minutes.

INSURANCE

Find a knowledgeable insurance broker who can help you with your business insurance. It may be the same person who handles your homeowner and your car insurance, since there are often savings when you combine policies. If your business is still very small, a knowledgeable broker can tell you whether your other policies will cover your needs until your business grows larger. Remember that liability coverage is an important part of your protection. Make sure that the agent knows what your marketing niche entails. She will know if you need to be covered at shows away from home or at weddings where you install the flowers. Discuss whether you need special coverage for edible or medicinal herb products.

STATE AND LOCAL SALES TAX

Be aware of regulations in your area and in other states where you go to sell. Especially at large events, tax agents may make the rounds to ensure that you are registered with the state. Registering with the state is a necessary nuisance, something to think about well in advance of an event. Usually it costs nothing to register, except time and frustration. Although I registered with the state of New York three years ago because I had a stand at the New York Flower Show, I haven't had an opportunity to go to the show since then. To keep my registration current, each quarter I must fill out a tax form declaring no income. Although I diligently follow the rules, marking zeros in all the appropriate boxes and mailing the form back, this quarter for some reason I got a notice that the state hadn't received my return, and I would soon be levied a hefty fine. I couldn't even say, "The check's in the mail," because no income, no check. Can I avoid a fine for zero taxes due? Stay tuned!

HEALTH REGULATIONS

If you sell culinary herbs, check with your state health department on regulations for products and display. I just returned from a large show where the booth of a major herb house was completely closed for three precious selling hours by the health department. The vendor was offering tastes of his herbal recipes in dip form, allowing customers to dip a cracker into a jar to scoop up some of the tasty treats. A regulation prohibits customers' fingers near the open jar of food and dipping by the customer, lest she take a bite and reinsert the bitten chip into the jar.

COMPUTERS FROM HEAVEN

Yes, there are people in the world who don't use computers for small businesses, but I strongly recommend that you not be among them. Although I protested loudly against the need for my first Macintosh, I became a total convert and must proselytize. Here are some of the main uses in your business.

Record Keeping

Simple programs like Managing Your Money, Managing Your Business, and Quicken will allow you to have immediate, accurate access to all of your accounts. Refer to your accounts for your own projections and planning. If you go to borrow money, your banker will be impressed with your businesslike approach. You will save money at tax time even if you don't do your own taxes, by handing the accountant in legible and comprehensible form everything she needs to complete your return.

Expenses are separated into categories. In addition to the usual, like advertising, postage, and equipment, I have a special category for garden expenses, like seeds, fertilizers, and plants. I want to know how much it is costing me to grow my flowers. Income is also broken into categories, and you are in charge of developing your own. If you teach and do workshops, write, give tours, and have home parties in addition to doing crafts shows, it's extremely helpful to know what percentage of your income derives from what source.

My retail sales are divided according to taxing unit, so sales in Philadelphia, which currently charges 7 percent tax, are separated from those in the rest of the state, which generally are 6 percent, and from New York City, where taxes currently are $8 1/4$ percent. To complicate matters further, the elegant straw hats trimmed with dried flowers and herbs fall as wearing apparel into the nontaxable category in Pennsylvania, but are fully taxed in New York City. When I need to submit quarterly sales tax returns, I can enter a computer command that will tell me my income in each category in each venue.

Computerized Mailing Lists

In addition to name, address, and zip code, enter a field coding where you acquired the name or any other special information. As an example, you could code LP for Long's Park Craft Festival in Lancaster, Pennsylvania. When you return to that show year after year, sort the mailing list for all the customers you gleaned from there and send them a reminder card to come and view your latest creations.

Devise a code for the media, which you will continually update, to sort for publicity purposes, news releases, and the like.

Sort your list by zip code when you want to save money and mail publicity fliers third class.

Graphic Design

Even if you pay an expert to have a logo and special graphics designed for your business, with the simplest of graphics programs, you can produce your own professional-looking fliers, invitations, newsletters, news releases, and other publicity items. Your promotional materials should be neat, accurate, beautifully designed, and of the quality that represents your craft. Save money by taking "camera ready" materials to your printer for large numbers of copies. For small quantities, print them out yourself on a high-quality printer.

If you have a graphics program but want more selection in illustrations, purchase books from the Dover or other clip art series, which are published for you to reproduce. Cut and paste by hand to your printed copy before you run off the quantity that you need. Also available are computer disks that contain additional herb and flower graphics. Check the classifieds of your favorite flower and herb journals for such opportunities. As a member of the Garden Writers Association of America, I regularly receive artwork from seed and bulb companies that is available for reproduction.

Signs

Whether you need large signs for sales and specials, price notices, or product descriptions, you can quickly and effectively print your own. Vary the size of the font and the type as necessary. Manually feed card stock or other special papers to produce a unique look.

Juried crafts and flower shows often require a slide of your dis-

BOOKS THAT HELP

There are many books that discuss the business side of business, a side in which crafters often have little interest. One particularly helpful book is *How to Open and Operate a Home-based Craft Business*, by Kenn Oberrecht. With any book, check the copyright date to see when it was written. Remember that tax laws and regulations change yearly, and any book is likely to be out of date about the very issues on which you need consultation. Many business books still in the bookstores were written before the popularity of home computers and thus don't advocate their use in keeping business records. Beware of taking outmoded advice, not only for pencil and paper bookkeeping, but on all tax matters. IRS and state regulations on deductions may be outmoded before a manuscript leaves an editor's desk.

Take a look at the current IRS pamphlets on regulations for business if you care to tackle them, or the yearly tax guides published by H & R Block and Lassers for up-to-date information. ❧

play as well as slides of your crafts. Judges seek professional-looking signs and notices, rather than scribbled or hand-printed ones. Your computer will help you seem like the professional you are.

Mail Order Catalog
If and when you decide to sell your products by mail order, use the computer for compiling the list, adding and deleting items, and changing prices as necessary.

Writing
When I wrote my first book, another lifetime and another career ago, I worked with a coauthor. I wrote longhand on a yellow legal

pad, double spaced, with a freshly sharpened #2 lead pencil. He typed at home on an Underwood manual typewriter. In the morning we brought in our various efforts to the psychology department secretary, who gamely retyped our outputs of the previous day. We edited and reedited each other's work, each draft requiring that the secretary retype. When all was ready, about ten drafts later, we shipped the manuscript to the publisher with a huge sigh.

Imagine my pleasure as I write this manuscript. I move sentences, paragraphs, and chapters with abandon. I delete verbiage, check my spelling, and search for the perfect synonym. I feel the way women must have felt when they changed from doing the wash in a stovetop boiler to using a gleaming white porcelain Bendix.

❧ WHERE TO GO FOR MORE HELP ❧

- State cooperative extension service
- State book of fairs and festivals; the American Automobile Association has this information available
- The business school at a local university or college, which often has assistance for small businesses
- Chamber of commerce, local or state branch
- Local merchants' association
- Local and state visitors bureau or tourist bureau
- Trade shows
- Trade associations
- U.S. Department of Agriculture and the state department of agriculture, for rules on herbal and food products and what you can make in the home. Check on rules for packaging and weights and measures of packaged goods.
- Small Business Administration for publications and individual help
- SCORE (Service Corps of Retired Executives) and the Active Corps of Executives for individual help

WHOLESALE PROMOTERS AND GIFT SHOWS

Americana Sampler
P.O. Box 160009
Nashville, TN 37216
(615) 227-2080
Kansas City Country Market, Overland Park, KS
Fort Washington Summer Market, Fort Washington, PA

Atlanta International Gift Mart
240 Peach Tree St., Ste. 2200
Atlanta, GA 30303
(404) 220-2200

Industry Productions of America
P.O. Box 27337
Los Angeles, CA 90027
(213) 962-5424
Beckman's Handcrafted Gift Show, Chicago, Dallas,
    and Los Angeles

LA Mart
1933 S. Broadway
Los Angeles, CA 90007
(800) LAMART4
California Gift Show, Los Angeles

George Little Management
10 Bank St., Ste. 1200
White Plains, NY 10606
(800) 272-SHOW
Boston Gift Show
Chicago Gift Show
New York International Gift Fair
New York Stationery Show
San Francisco International Gift Fair
Washington Gift Show, Washington, DC

Reber-Friel Co.
221 King Manor Dr.
King of Prussia, PA 19406
(610) 272-4020
Eastern Regional Gift Show, Valley Forge, PA

The Rosen Group
Ste. 300 Mill Center
3000 Chestnut Ave.
Baltimore, MD 21211
(410) 889-2933
Buyers Market of American Craft, Boston and Philadelphia

❧ FLOWER AND HERB SHOWS ❧

Chelsea America Flower Show
Delray Beach, FL
(407) 478-9395

Cincinnati Flower Show
Cincinnati Horticultural
	Society
124 Convention Ave.
Cincinnati, OH 45202
(513) 579-0259

Cleveland Flower Festival
Cleveland Botanical Gardens
11030 East Blvd.
Cleveland, OH 44106
(216) 721-1695

Dallas Spring Home and
	Garden Show
Dallas, TX
(214) 680-9995

New England Spring Flower
	Show
Massachusetts Horticultural
	Society
300 Massachusetts Ave.
Boston, MA 02115
(617) 536-9280

New York Flower Show
New York Horticultural Society
128 W. 58th St.
New York, NY 10019
(212) 757-0915

Northwest Flower and Garden
	Show
1515 N.W. 51st
Seattle, WA 98107
(206) 789-5333

Philadelphia Flower Show
Pennsylvania Horticultural
	Society
325 Walnut St.
Philadelphia, PA
(215) 625-8253

Rhode Island Spring Flower
and Garden Show
Providence, RI
George Little Management
(800) 272-SHOW

San Francisco Landscape
Garden Show
Friends of Parks and
Recreation
McLaren Lodge, Golden Gate
Park
San Francisco, CA
(415) 750-5108

Southeastern Flower Show
Atlanta Botanical Gardens
1345 Piedmont Ave.
Atlanta, GA 30309
(404) 876-5859

American Crafts Retailers
Association
P.O. Box 653
Cockeysville, MD 21030
(410) 321-7112

Association of Bridal
Consultants
200 Chestnutland Rd.
New Milford, CT 06776-2521
(203) 355-0464

Association of Specialty Cut
Flower Growers
P.O. Box 268
Oberlin, OH 44074
(216) 884-5716

Authors Guild
330 W. 42nd St.
New York, NY 10036
(212) 563-5904

Garden Writers Association
of America
10210 Leatherleaf Court
Manassas, VA 22111
(703) 257-0213

Herb Society of America
9019 Kirtland Chardon Rd.
Mentor, OH 44060

International Herb Growers &
Marketers Association
1202 Allanson Rd.
Mundelein, IL 60060
(708) 949-4372

National Education Center for
Women in Business
Seton Hill College
Seton Hill Dr.
Greensburg, PA 15601
(800) NECWB-4-U

❧ REFERENCES ❧

On Writing

Appelbaum, Judith. *How to Get Happily Published*. 4th ed. New York: Harper-Collins, 1992. Important reading for all new authors and would-be authors. Ideas for marketing your book and yourself. Agents, contracts, editing, and all critical topics.

Publishers Weekly. News of the publishing world. If you plan to write, it pays to know what's going on.

Writer's Market: Where & How to Sell What You Write. Cincinnati: Writers Digest Books, published yearly. The title says it all. Especially helpful for writers seeking to place material in periodicals.

On Crafts

The Craft Report: The News Monthly for Professionals. By subscription. Call (800) 777-7098; single issues at specialized newsstands and bookstores. Listings of important wholesale and retail shows and fairs, workshops, and conferences. Includes articles on designing your booth, successful selling, loans to very small businesses, handling accounts, and law for craftspeople. Timely information reflects recent changes in IRS regulations and other business-related topics. It is *not* about the flower and herb crafts business, but articles are highly relevant.

Crafting as a Business. Baltimore: The Rosen Group: Source book for top shows, fairs, galleries, resources, and pricing from a major show promoter. Not specific to flower and herb crafts.

Gifts & Decorative Accessories. 51 Madison Ave., New York, NY 10010; (212) 689-4411. Monthly magazine of the wholesale gift industry, trends and forecasts, profitable ideas, retailing, design, display, sales, markets, shows, and buyers directory.

Giftware News. P.O. Box 5398, Deptford, NJ 08096; (609) 277-0798. Published thirteen times a year; news of the wholesale gift industry, new products, markets, shows, and trends.

The Harris List. P.O. Box 142, La Veta, CO 81055; (719) 742-3146. Published each year; ratings and listings of approximately 180 of the top arts and crafts shows in the country. Helps in deciding which shows are for you. Many of the shows will not accept flower and herb crafts, but those that do are important. The list is developed from recommendations of working artists.

Niche Magazine. 3000 Chestnut Ave., Suite 300, Baltimore, MD 21211; (800) CRAFT93. Trade magazine for crafts retailers. Not specific to flower and herb business but many relevant topics.

On Flowers and Herbs

The Cut Flower Quarterly. P.O. Box 268, Oberlin, OH 44074; (216) 774-2887.

Flowers &. Teleflora Plaza, Suite 118, 12233 W. Olympic Blvd., Los Angeles, CA 90064; (310) 826-5253. Published monthly for professional florists; available by subscription. Design and color trends, pricing, marketing, statistics on the floral trade.

Growing for Market. P.O. Box 3747, Lawrence, KS 66046. Monthly publication that includes information for cut and dried flower growers, along with fruit and vegetable growers.

Hawken, Paul. *Growing a Business.* NY: Simon & Schuster, 1988. Inspirational material from a master in highly readable form.

Herb Companion. Interweave Press, 201 E. Fourth St., Loveland, CO 80537; (303) 669-7672. Ads, calendar of coming events by state, articles on growing, history, and cooking.

The Herb Quarterly. P.O. Box 689, San Anselmo, CA 94960. Display and classified ads, workshops, programs, and symposia listed by state, articles on growing, design, history, and uses.

The Herbal Connection. P.O. Box 245, Silver Spring, PA 17575; (717) 393-3295. Bimonthly newsletter with strong business orientation.

The Herbal Green Pages: An Herbal Resource Guide. The Herb Growing & Marketing Network, P.O. Box 245, Silver Spring, PA 17575; (717) 393-3295. Resources by name and state, book publishers and dealers, associations and societies, periodicals, botanical gardens, and suppliers. Excellent and essential all-purpose resource. List your business free in the directory.

Kowalchik, Claire, and William H. Hylton, eds. *Rodale's Illustrated Encyclopedia of Herbs.* Emmaus, PA: Rodale Press, 1987. Compendium of highly useful information on hundreds of herbs.

Platt, Ellen Spector. *Flower Crafts: A Step-by-Step Guide to Growing, Drying & Decorating with Flowers.* Emmaus, PA: Rodale Press, 1993. Best flowers to grow for drying and how to dry them. Fifty original designs.

————.*Wreaths, Arrangements & Basket Decorations*. Emmaus, PA: Rodale Press, 1994. Step-by-step instructions for making fifty original designs. Advice on using colors to highlight designs, keeping the colors, and changing colors naturally.

————.*The Ultimate Wreath Book*. Emmaus, PA: Rodale Press, 1995. Over 150 ideas for wreaths of all sizes, shapes, and themes. Explicit instructions.

Professional Floral Design. American Floral Service, 3737 N.W. 34th St., Oklahoma City, OK, 73112. Published six times a year; full color design magazine for florists using fresh silk and dried materials. Yearly wedding and holiday issues. Discussion of design principles for each arrangement. Highly instructive.

Reppert, Bertha. *Growing Your Herb Business*, Pownal, VT: Storey, 1994. Insights garnered from personal experience by one of the originals in the herb business. Emphasis on retail stores.

Sturdivant, Lee. *Herbs for Sale*. Friday Harbor, WA: San Juan Naturals, 1994.

On Business

The Business of Herbs. Northwind Farm Publications, R.R. 2 Box 246, Shevlin, MN 56676; (218) 657-2478. A bimonthly bulletin packed with information for growers and marketers. They also publish a complete directory of herb farms and herb-related businesses called *The Herb Resource Directory*.

Edwards, Paul, Sarah Edwards, and Laura Clampitt Douglas. *Getting Business to Come to You*. New York: Putnam's Sons, 1991.

Oberrecht, Kenn. *How to Operate a Home-Based Craft Business*. Old Saybrook, CT: Globe Pequot Press, 1994. Thorough discussion of the business side of the crafts business. Writing is clear and helpful.

Siegel, Gonnie McClung. *How to Advertise and Promote Your Small Business*. New York: Wiley Press, 1978. Slightly out of date because it has no discussions of computer graphics and desktop printing, but the advertising principles are still valuable.

Small Business Administration Publications Guide. Updated regularly. Call SBA for the latest listing with prices. The number of your nearest regional office is available from telephone information.

Some Helpful Hints on Pricing Craft Work. 700 Orange St., Wilmington, DE 19801; (302) 656-2209. A special study by *The Crafts Report*.

❦ INDEX ❦